The Party Planning Checklist10

ISBN-13: 978-1544215624

ISBN-10: 1544215622

birthday party planner

to do:	to buy:	party schedule:
☐ select party date	☐ invitations	start _____
☐ make guest list	☐ stamps	0:15 _____
☐ address invitations	☐ paper cups	0:30 _____
☐ mail invitations	☐ paper plates	0:45 _____
☐ plan party theme	☐ napkins	1:00 _____
☐ decide on favors	☐ tablecloth	1:15 _____
☐ order birthday cake	☐ utensils	1:30 _____
☐ plan entertainment	☐ balloons	1:45 _____
☐ contact entertainers	☐ streamers/signs	2:00 _____
☐ buy food, décor items	☐ place cards	2:15 _____
☐ prepare house for party	☐ favors/party bags	2:30 _____
☐ decorate	☐	2:45 _____
☐	☐	3:00 _____
☐	☐	_____
☐ clean –up	☐	_____
☐ write thank you notes	☐	_____
☐ mail thank you notes	☐	_____

notes:	party info:
_____	date:_____
_____	time:_____
_____	theme:_____
_____	cake:_____
_____	favors: _____
_____	entertainment:

birthday party planner

to do:	to buy:	party schedule:
☐ select party date	☐ invitations	start _____
☐ make guest list	☐ stamps	0:15 _____
☐ address invitations	☐ paper cups	0:30 _____
☐ mail invitations	☐ paper plates	0:45 _____
☐ plan party theme	☐ napkins	1:00 _____
☐ decide on favors	☐ tablecloth	1:15 _____
☐ order birthday cake	☐ utensils	1:30 _____
☐ plan entertainment	☐ balloons	1:45 _____
☐ contact entertainers	☐ streamers/signs	2:00 _____
☐ buy food, décor items	☐ place cards	2:15 _____
☐ prepare house for party	☐ favors/party bags	2:30 _____
☐ decorate	☐	2:45 _____
☐	☐	3:00 _____
☐	☐	_____
☐ clean –up	☐	_____
☐ write thank you notes	☐	_____
☐ mail thank you notes	☐	_____

notes:	party info:
_____	date:_____
_____	time:_____
_____	theme:_____
_____	cake:_____
_____	favors: _____
_____	entertainment:

birthday party planner

to do:	to buy:	party schedule:
☐ select party date	☐ invitations	start _____
☐ make guest list	☐ stamps	0:15 _____
☐ address invitations	☐ paper cups	0:30 _____
☐ mail invitations	☐ paper plates	0:45 _____
☐ plan party theme	☐ napkins	1:00 _____
☐ decide on favors	☐ tablecloth	1:15 _____
☐ order birthday cake	☐ utensils	1:30 _____
☐ plan entertainment	☐ balloons	1:45 _____
☐ contact entertainers	☐ streamers/signs	2:00 _____
☐ buy food, décor items	☐ place cards	2:15 _____
☐ prepare house for party	☐ favors/party bags	2:30 _____
☐ decorate	☐	2:45 _____
☐	☐	3:00 _____
☐	☐	_____
☐ clean –up	☐	_____
☐ write thank you notes	☐	_____
☐ mail thank you notes	☐	_____

notes:	party info:
_____	date:_____
_____	time:_____
_____	theme:_____
_____	cake:_____
_____	favors: _____
_____	entertainment:

birthday party planner

to do:	to buy:	party schedule:
☐ select party date	☐ invitations	start _____
☐ make guest list	☐ stamps	0:15 _____
☐ address invitations	☐ paper cups	0:30 _____
☐ mail invitations	☐ paper plates	0:45 _____
☐ plan party theme	☐ napkins	1:00 _____
☐ decide on favors	☐ tablecloth	1:15 _____
☐ order birthday cake	☐ utensils	1:30 _____
☐ plan entertainment	☐ balloons	1:45 _____
☐ contact entertainers	☐ streamers/signs	2:00 _____
☐ buy food, décor items	☐ place cards	2:15 _____
☐ prepare house for party	☐ favors/party bags	2:30 _____
☐ decorate	☐	2:45 _____
☐	☐	3:00 _____
☐	☐	_____
☐ clean –up	☐	_____
☐ write thank you notes	☐	_____
☐ mail thank you notes	☐	_____

notes:	party info:
_____	date:_____
_____	time:_____
_____	theme:_____
_____	cake:_____
_____	favors: _____
_____	entertainment:

birthday party planner

to do:	to buy:	party schedule:
☐ select party date	☐ invitations	start _____
☐ make guest list	☐ stamps	0:15 _____
☐ address invitations	☐ paper cups	0:30 _____
☐ mail invitations	☐ paper plates	0:45 _____
☐ plan party theme	☐ napkins	1:00 _____
☐ decide on favors	☐ tablecloth	1:15 _____
☐ order birthday cake	☐ utensils	1:30 _____
☐ plan entertainment	☐ balloons	1:45 _____
☐ contact entertainers	☐ streamers/signs	2:00 _____
☐ buy food, décor items	☐ place cards	2:15 _____
☐ prepare house for party	☐ favors/party bags	2:30 _____
☐ decorate	☐	2:45 _____
☐	☐	3:00 _____
☐	☐	_____
☐ clean –up	☐	_____
☐ write thank you notes	☐	_____
☐ mail thank you notes	☐	_____

notes:	party info:
_____	date:_____
_____	time:_____
_____	theme:_____
_____	cake:_____
_____	favors: _____
_____	entertainment:

birthday party planner

to do:	to buy:	party schedule:
☐ select party date	☐ invitations	start _____
☐ make guest list	☐ stamps	0:15 _____
☐ address invitations	☐ paper cups	0:30 _____
☐ mail invitations	☐ paper plates	0:45 _____
☐ plan party theme	☐ napkins	1:00 _____
☐ decide on favors	☐ tablecloth	1:15 _____
☐ order birthday cake	☐ utensils	1:30 _____
☐ plan entertainment	☐ balloons	1:45 _____
☐ contact entertainers	☐ streamers/signs	2:00 _____
☐ buy food, décor items	☐ place cards	2:15 _____
☐ prepare house for party	☐ favors/party bags	2:30 _____
☐ decorate	☐	2:45 _____
☐	☐	3:00 _____
☐	☐	_____
☐ clean –up	☐	_____
☐ write thank you notes	☐	_____
☐ mail thank you notes	☐	_____

notes:	party info:
_____	date:_____
_____	time:_____
_____	theme:_____
_____	cake:_____
_____	favors: _____
_____	entertainment:

birthday party planner

to do:	to buy:	party schedule:
☐ select party date	☐ invitations	start _____
☐ make guest list	☐ stamps	0:15 _____
☐ address invitations	☐ paper cups	0:30 _____
☐ mail invitations	☐ paper plates	0:45 _____
☐ plan party theme	☐ napkins	1:00 _____
☐ decide on favors	☐ tablecloth	1:15 _____
☐ order birthday cake	☐ utensils	1:30 _____
☐ plan entertainment	☐ balloons	1:45 _____
☐ contact entertainers	☐ streamers/signs	2:00 _____
☐ buy food, décor items	☐ place cards	2:15 _____
☐ prepare house for party	☐ favors/party bags	2:30 _____
☐ decorate	☐	2:45 _____
☐	☐	3:00 _____
☐	☐	_____
☐ clean –up	☐	_____
☐ write thank you notes	☐	_____
☐ mail thank you notes	☐	_____

notes:	party info:
_____	date:_____
_____	time:_____
_____	theme:_____
_____	cake:_____
_____	favors: _____
_____	entertainment:

birthday party planner

to do:	to buy:	party schedule:
☐ select party date	☐ invitations	start _____
☐ make guest list	☐ stamps	0:15 _____
☐ address invitations	☐ paper cups	0:30 _____
☐ mail invitations	☐ paper plates	0:45 _____
☐ plan party theme	☐ napkins	1:00 _____
☐ decide on favors	☐ tablecloth	1:15 _____
☐ order birthday cake	☐ utensils	1:30 _____
☐ plan entertainment	☐ balloons	1:45 _____
☐ contact entertainers	☐ streamers/signs	2:00 _____
☐ buy food, décor items	☐ place cards	2:15 _____
☐ prepare house for party	☐ favors/party bags	2:30 _____
☐ decorate	☐	2:45 _____
☐	☐	3:00 _____
☐	☐	_____
☐ clean –up	☐	_____
☐ write thank you notes	☐	_____
☐ mail thank you notes	☐	_____
		_____

notes:	party info:
_____	date:_____
_____	time:_____
_____	theme:_____
_____	cake:_____
_____	favors: _____
_____	entertainment:

birthday party planner

to do:	to buy:	party schedule:
☐ select party date	☐ invitations	start _____
☐ make guest list	☐ stamps	0:15 _____
☐ address invitations	☐ paper cups	0:30 _____
☐ mail invitations	☐ paper plates	0:45 _____
☐ plan party theme	☐ napkins	1:00 _____
☐ decide on favors	☐ tablecloth	1:15 _____
☐ order birthday cake	☐ utensils	1:30 _____
☐ plan entertainment	☐ balloons	1:45 _____
☐ contact entertainers	☐ streamers/signs	2:00 _____
☐ buy food, décor items	☐ place cards	2:15 _____
☐ prepare house for party	☐ favors/party bags	2:30 _____
☐ decorate	☐	2:45 _____
☐	☐	3:00 _____
☐	☐	_____
☐ clean –up	☐	_____
☐ write thank you notes	☐	_____
☐ mail thank you notes	☐	_____

notes:	party info:
_____	date:_____
_____	time:_____
_____	theme:_____
_____	cake:_____
_____	favors: _____
_____	entertainment:

birthday party planner

to do:	to buy:	party schedule:
☐ select party date	☐ invitations	start _____
☐ make guest list	☐ stamps	0:15 _____
☐ address invitations	☐ paper cups	0:30 _____
☐ mail invitations	☐ paper plates	0:45 _____
☐ plan party theme	☐ napkins	1:00 _____
☐ decide on favors	☐ tablecloth	1:15 _____
☐ order birthday cake	☐ utensils	1:30 _____
☐ plan entertainment	☐ balloons	1:45 _____
☐ contact entertainers	☐ streamers/signs	2:00 _____
☐ buy food, décor items	☐ place cards	2:15 _____
☐ prepare house for party	☐ favors/party bags	2:30 _____
☐ decorate	☐	2:45 _____
☐	☐	3:00 _____
☐	☐	_____
☐ clean –up	☐	_____
☐ write thank you notes	☐	_____
☐ mail thank you notes	☐	_____

notes:	party info:
_____	date:_____
_____	time:_____
_____	theme:_____
_____	cake:_____
_____	favors: _____
_____	entertainment:

birthday party planner

to do:	to buy:	party schedule:
☐ select party date	☐ invitations	start _____
☐ make guest list	☐ stamps	0:15 _____
☐ address invitations	☐ paper cups	0:30 _____
☐ mail invitations	☐ paper plates	0:45 _____
☐ plan party theme	☐ napkins	1:00 _____
☐ decide on favors	☐ tablecloth	1:15 _____
☐ order birthday cake	☐ utensils	1:30 _____
☐ plan entertainment	☐ balloons	1:45 _____
☐ contact entertainers	☐ streamers/signs	2:00 _____
☐ buy food, décor items	☐ place cards	2:15 _____
☐ prepare house for party	☐ favors/party bags	2:30 _____
☐ decorate	☐	2:45 _____
☐	☐	3:00 _____
☐	☐	_____
☐ clean –up	☐	_____
☐ write thank you notes	☐	_____
☐ mail thank you notes	☐	_____

notes:	party info:
_____	date:_____
_____	time:_____
_____	theme:_____
_____	cake:_____
_____	favors: _____
_____	entertainment:

birthday party planner

to do:	to buy:	party schedule:
☐ select party date	☐ invitations	start _____
☐ make guest list	☐ stamps	0:15 _____
☐ address invitations	☐ paper cups	0:30 _____
☐ mail invitations	☐ paper plates	0:45 _____
☐ plan party theme	☐ napkins	1:00 _____
☐ decide on favors	☐ tablecloth	1:15 _____
☐ order birthday cake	☐ utensils	1:30 _____
☐ plan entertainment	☐ balloons	1:45 _____
☐ contact entertainers	☐ streamers/signs	2:00 _____
☐ buy food, décor items	☐ place cards	2:15 _____
☐ prepare house for party	☐ favors/party bags	2:30 _____
☐ decorate	☐	2:45 _____
☐	☐	3:00 _____
☐	☐	_____
☐ clean –up	☐	_____
☐ write thank you notes	☐	_____
☐ mail thank you notes	☐	_____

notes:	party info:
_____	date:_____
_____	time:_____
_____	theme:_____
_____	cake:_____
_____	favors: _____
_____	entertainment:

birthday party planner

to do:	to buy:	party schedule:
☐ select party date	☐ invitations	start _____
☐ make guest list	☐ stamps	0:15 _____
☐ address invitations	☐ paper cups	0:30 _____
☐ mail invitations	☐ paper plates	0:45 _____
☐ plan party theme	☐ napkins	1:00 _____
☐ decide on favors	☐ tablecloth	1:15 _____
☐ order birthday cake	☐ utensils	1:30 _____
☐ plan entertainment	☐ balloons	1:45 _____
☐ contact entertainers	☐ streamers/signs	2:00 _____
☐ buy food, décor items	☐ place cards	2:15 _____
☐ prepare house for party	☐ favors/party bags	2:30 _____
☐ decorate	☐	2:45 _____
☐	☐	3:00 _____
☐	☐	_____
☐ clean –up	☐	_____
☐ write thank you notes	☐	_____
☐ mail thank you notes	☐	_____

notes:	party info:
_____	date:_____
_____	time:_____
_____	theme:_____
_____	cake:_____
_____	favors: _____
_____	entertainment:

birthday party planner

to do:	to buy:	party schedule:
☐ select party date	☐ invitations	start _____
☐ make guest list	☐ stamps	0:15 _____
☐ address invitations	☐ paper cups	0:30 _____
☐ mail invitations	☐ paper plates	0:45 _____
☐ plan party theme	☐ napkins	1:00 _____
☐ decide on favors	☐ tablecloth	1:15 _____
☐ order birthday cake	☐ utensils	1:30 _____
☐ plan entertainment	☐ balloons	1:45 _____
☐ contact entertainers	☐ streamers/signs	2:00 _____
☐ buy food, décor items	☐ place cards	2:15 _____
☐ prepare house for party	☐ favors/party bags	2:30 _____
☐ decorate	☐	2:45 _____
☐	☐	3:00 _____
☐	☐	_____
☐ clean –up	☐	_____
☐ write thank you notes	☐	_____
☐ mail thank you notes	☐	_____

notes:	party info:
_____	date:_____
_____	time:_____
_____	theme:_____
_____	cake:_____
_____	favors: _____
_____	entertainment:

birthday party planner

to do:	to buy:	party schedule:
☐ select party date	☐ invitations	start _____
☐ make guest list	☐ stamps	0:15 _____
☐ address invitations	☐ paper cups	0:30 _____
☐ mail invitations	☐ paper plates	0:45 _____
☐ plan party theme	☐ napkins	1:00 _____
☐ decide on favors	☐ tablecloth	1:15 _____
☐ order birthday cake	☐ utensils	1:30 _____
☐ plan entertainment	☐ balloons	1:45 _____
☐ contact entertainers	☐ streamers/signs	2:00 _____
☐ buy food, décor items	☐ place cards	2:15 _____
☐ prepare house for party	☐ favors/party bags	2:30 _____
☐ decorate	☐	2:45 _____
☐	☐	3:00 _____
☐	☐	_____
☐ clean –up	☐	_____
☐ write thank you notes	☐	_____
☐ mail thank you notes	☐	_____

notes:	party info:
_____	date:_____
_____	time:_____
_____	theme:_____
_____	cake:_____
_____	favors: _____
_____	entertainment:

birthday party planner

to do:	to buy:	party schedule:
☐ select party date	☐ invitations	start _____
☐ make guest list	☐ stamps	0:15 _____
☐ address invitations	☐ paper cups	0:30 _____
☐ mail invitations	☐ paper plates	0:45 _____
☐ plan party theme	☐ napkins	1:00 _____
☐ decide on favors	☐ tablecloth	1:15 _____
☐ order birthday cake	☐ utensils	1:30 _____
☐ plan entertainment	☐ balloons	1:45 _____
☐ contact entertainers	☐ streamers/signs	2:00 _____
☐ buy food, décor items	☐ place cards	2:15 _____
☐ prepare house for party	☐ favors/party bags	2:30 _____
☐ decorate	☐	2:45 _____
☐	☐	3:00 _____
☐	☐	_____
☐ clean –up	☐	_____
☐ write thank you notes	☐	_____
☐ mail thank you notes	☐	_____

notes:	party info:
_____	date:_____
_____	time:_____
_____	theme:_____
_____	cake:_____
_____	favors: _____
_____	entertainment:

birthday party planner

to do:	to buy:	party schedule:
☐ select party date	☐ invitations	start _____
☐ make guest list	☐ stamps	0:15 _____
☐ address invitations	☐ paper cups	0:30 _____
☐ mail invitations	☐ paper plates	0:45 _____
☐ plan party theme	☐ napkins	1:00 _____
☐ decide on favors	☐ tablecloth	1:15 _____
☐ order birthday cake	☐ utensils	1:30 _____
☐ plan entertainment	☐ balloons	1:45 _____
☐ contact entertainers	☐ streamers/signs	2:00 _____
☐ buy food, décor items	☐ place cards	2:15 _____
☐ prepare house for party	☐ favors/party bags	2:30 _____
☐ decorate	☐	2:45 _____
☐	☐	3:00 _____
☐	☐	_____
☐ clean –up	☐	_____
☐ write thank you notes	☐	_____
☐ mail thank you notes	☐	_____

notes:	party info:
_____	date:_____
_____	time:_____
_____	theme:_____
_____	cake:_____
_____	favors: _____
_____	entertainment:

birthday party planner

to do:	to buy:	party schedule:
☐ select party date	☐ invitations	start _____
☐ make guest list	☐ stamps	0:15 _____
☐ address invitations	☐ paper cups	0:30 _____
☐ mail invitations	☐ paper plates	0:45 _____
☐ plan party theme	☐ napkins	1:00 _____
☐ decide on favors	☐ tablecloth	1:15 _____
☐ order birthday cake	☐ utensils	1:30 _____
☐ plan entertainment	☐ balloons	1:45 _____
☐ contact entertainers	☐ streamers/signs	2:00 _____
☐ buy food, décor items	☐ place cards	2:15 _____
☐ prepare house for party	☐ favors/party bags	2:30 _____
☐ decorate	☐	2:45 _____
☐	☐	3:00 _____
☐	☐	_____
☐ clean –up	☐	_____
☐ write thank you notes	☐	_____
☐ mail thank you notes	☐	_____

notes:	party info:
_____	date:_____
_____	time:_____
_____	theme:_____
_____	cake:_____
_____	favors: _____
_____	entertainment:

birthday party planner

to do:	to buy:	party schedule:
☐ select party date	☐ invitations	start _____
☐ make guest list	☐ stamps	0:15 _____
☐ address invitations	☐ paper cups	0:30 _____
☐ mail invitations	☐ paper plates	0:45 _____
☐ plan party theme	☐ napkins	1:00 _____
☐ decide on favors	☐ tablecloth	1:15 _____
☐ order birthday cake	☐ utensils	1:30 _____
☐ plan entertainment	☐ balloons	1:45 _____
☐ contact entertainers	☐ streamers/signs	2:00 _____
☐ buy food, décor items	☐ place cards	2:15 _____
☐ prepare house for party	☐ favors/party bags	2:30 _____
☐ decorate	☐	2:45 _____
☐	☐	3:00 _____
☐	☐	_____
☐ clean –up	☐	_____
☐ write thank you notes	☐	_____
☐ mail thank you notes	☐	_____

notes:	party info:
_____	date:_____
_____	time:_____
_____	theme:_____
_____	cake:_____
_____	favors: _____
_____	entertainment:

birthday party planner

to do:	to buy:	party schedule:
☐ select party date	☐ invitations	start _____
☐ make guest list	☐ stamps	0:15 _____
☐ address invitations	☐ paper cups	0:30 _____
☐ mail invitations	☐ paper plates	0:45 _____
☐ plan party theme	☐ napkins	1:00 _____
☐ decide on favors	☐ tablecloth	1:15 _____
☐ order birthday cake	☐ utensils	1:30 _____
☐ plan entertainment	☐ balloons	1:45 _____
☐ contact entertainers	☐ streamers/signs	2:00 _____
☐ buy food, décor items	☐ place cards	2:15 _____
☐ prepare house for party	☐ favors/party bags	2:30 _____
☐ decorate	☐	2:45 _____
☐	☐	3:00 _____
☐	☐	_____
☐ clean –up	☐	_____
☐ write thank you notes	☐	_____
☐ mail thank you notes	☐	_____

notes:	party info:
_____	date:_____
_____	time:_____
_____	theme:_____
_____	cake:_____
_____	favors: _____
_____	entertainment:

birthday party planner

to do:	to buy:	party schedule:
☐ select party date	☐ invitations	start _____
☐ make guest list	☐ stamps	0:15 _____
☐ address invitations	☐ paper cups	0:30 _____
☐ mail invitations	☐ paper plates	0:45 _____
☐ plan party theme	☐ napkins	1:00 _____
☐ decide on favors	☐ tablecloth	1:15 _____
☐ order birthday cake	☐ utensils	1:30 _____
☐ plan entertainment	☐ balloons	1:45 _____
☐ contact entertainers	☐ streamers/signs	2:00 _____
☐ buy food, décor items	☐ place cards	2:15 _____
☐ prepare house for party	☐ favors/party bags	2:30 _____
☐ decorate	☐	2:45 _____
☐	☐	3:00 _____
☐	☐	_____
☐ clean –up	☐	_____
☐ write thank you notes	☐	_____
☐ mail thank you notes	☐	_____
		_____

notes:	party info:
_____	date:_____
_____	time:_____
_____	theme:_____
_____	cake:_____
_____	favors: _____
_____	entertainment:

birthday party planner

to do:	to buy:	party schedule:
☐ select party date	☐ invitations	start _____
☐ make guest list	☐ stamps	0:15 _____
☐ address invitations	☐ paper cups	0:30 _____
☐ mail invitations	☐ paper plates	0:45 _____
☐ plan party theme	☐ napkins	1:00 _____
☐ decide on favors	☐ tablecloth	1:15 _____
☐ order birthday cake	☐ utensils	1:30 _____
☐ plan entertainment	☐ balloons	1:45 _____
☐ contact entertainers	☐ streamers/signs	2:00 _____
☐ buy food, décor items	☐ place cards	2:15 _____
☐ prepare house for party	☐ favors/party bags	2:30 _____
☐ decorate	☐	2:45 _____
☐	☐	3:00 _____
☐	☐	_____
☐ clean –up	☐	_____
☐ write thank you notes	☐	_____
☐ mail thank you notes	☐	_____

notes:	party info:
_____	date:_____
_____	time:_____
_____	theme:_____
_____	cake:_____
_____	favors: _____
_____	entertainment:

birthday party planner

to do:	to buy:	party schedule:
☐ select party date	☐ invitations	start _____
☐ make guest list	☐ stamps	0:15 _____
☐ address invitations	☐ paper cups	0:30 _____
☐ mail invitations	☐ paper plates	0:45 _____
☐ plan party theme	☐ napkins	1:00 _____
☐ decide on favors	☐ tablecloth	1:15 _____
☐ order birthday cake	☐ utensils	1:30 _____
☐ plan entertainment	☐ balloons	1:45 _____
☐ contact entertainers	☐ streamers/signs	2:00 _____
☐ buy food, décor items	☐ place cards	2:15 _____
☐ prepare house for party	☐ favors/party bags	2:30 _____
☐ decorate	☐	2:45 _____
☐	☐	3:00 _____
☐	☐	_____
☐ clean –up	☐	_____
☐ write thank you notes	☐	_____
☐ mail thank you notes	☐	_____

notes:	party info:
_____	date:_____
_____	time:_____
_____	theme:_____
_____	cake:_____
_____	favors: _____
_____	entertainment:

birthday party planner

to do:	to buy:	party schedule:
☐ select party date	☐ invitations	start _____
☐ make guest list	☐ stamps	0:15 _____
☐ address invitations	☐ paper cups	0:30 _____
☐ mail invitations	☐ paper plates	0:45 _____
☐ plan party theme	☐ napkins	1:00 _____
☐ decide on favors	☐ tablecloth	1:15 _____
☐ order birthday cake	☐ utensils	1:30 _____
☐ plan entertainment	☐ balloons	1:45 _____
☐ contact entertainers	☐ streamers/signs	2:00 _____
☐ buy food, décor items	☐ place cards	2:15 _____
☐ prepare house for party	☐ favors/party bags	2:30 _____
☐ decorate	☐	2:45 _____
☐	☐	3:00 _____
☐	☐	_____
☐ clean –up	☐	_____
☐ write thank you notes	☐	_____
☐ mail thank you notes	☐	_____

notes:	party info:
_____	date:_____
_____	time:_____
_____	theme:_____
_____	cake:_____
_____	favors: _____
_____	entertainment:

birthday party planner

to do:	to buy:	party schedule:
☐ select party date	☐ invitations	start _____
☐ make guest list	☐ stamps	0:15 _____
☐ address invitations	☐ paper cups	0:30 _____
☐ mail invitations	☐ paper plates	0:45 _____
☐ plan party theme	☐ napkins	1:00 _____
☐ decide on favors	☐ tablecloth	1:15 _____
☐ order birthday cake	☐ utensils	1:30 _____
☐ plan entertainment	☐ balloons	1:45 _____
☐ contact entertainers	☐ streamers/signs	2:00 _____
☐ buy food, décor items	☐ place cards	2:15 _____
☐ prepare house for party	☐ favors/party bags	2:30 _____
☐ decorate	☐	2:45 _____
☐	☐	3:00 _____
☐	☐	_____
☐ clean –up	☐	_____
☐ write thank you notes	☐	_____
☐ mail thank you notes	☐	_____

notes:	party info:
_____	date:_____
_____	time:_____
_____	theme:_____
_____	cake:_____
_____	favors: _____
_____	entertainment:

birthday party planner

to do:	to buy:	party schedule:
☐ select party date	☐ invitations	start _____
☐ make guest list	☐ stamps	0:15 _____
☐ address invitations	☐ paper cups	0:30 _____
☐ mail invitations	☐ paper plates	0:45 _____
☐ plan party theme	☐ napkins	1:00 _____
☐ decide on favors	☐ tablecloth	1:15 _____
☐ order birthday cake	☐ utensils	1:30 _____
☐ plan entertainment	☐ balloons	1:45 _____
☐ contact entertainers	☐ streamers/signs	2:00 _____
☐ buy food, décor items	☐ place cards	2:15 _____
☐ prepare house for party	☐ favors/party bags	2:30 _____
☐ decorate	☐	2:45 _____
☐	☐	3:00 _____
☐	☐	_____
☐ clean –up	☐	_____
☐ write thank you notes	☐	_____
☐ mail thank you notes	☐	_____

notes:	party info:
_____	date:_____
_____	time:_____
_____	theme:_____
_____	cake:_____
_____	favors: _____
_____	entertainment:

birthday party planner

to do:	to buy:	party schedule:
☐ select party date	☐ invitations	start _____
☐ make guest list	☐ stamps	0:15 _____
☐ address invitations	☐ paper cups	0:30 _____
☐ mail invitations	☐ paper plates	0:45 _____
☐ plan party theme	☐ napkins	1:00 _____
☐ decide on favors	☐ tablecloth	1:15 _____
☐ order birthday cake	☐ utensils	1:30 _____
☐ plan entertainment	☐ balloons	1:45 _____
☐ contact entertainers	☐ streamers/signs	2:00 _____
☐ buy food, décor items	☐ place cards	2:15 _____
☐ prepare house for party	☐ favors/party bags	2:30 _____
☐ decorate	☐	2:45 _____
☐	☐	3:00 _____
☐	☐	_____
☐ clean –up	☐	_____
☐ write thank you notes	☐	_____
☐ mail thank you notes	☐	_____

notes:	party info:
_____	date:_____
_____	time:_____
_____	theme:_____
_____	cake:_____
_____	favors: _____
_____	entertainment:

birthday party planner

to do:	to buy:	party schedule:
☐ select party date	☐ invitations	start _____
☐ make guest list	☐ stamps	0:15 _____
☐ address invitations	☐ paper cups	0:30 _____
☐ mail invitations	☐ paper plates	0:45 _____
☐ plan party theme	☐ napkins	1:00 _____
☐ decide on favors	☐ tablecloth	1:15 _____
☐ order birthday cake	☐ utensils	1:30 _____
☐ plan entertainment	☐ balloons	1:45 _____
☐ contact entertainers	☐ streamers/signs	2:00 _____
☐ buy food, décor items	☐ place cards	2:15 _____
☐ prepare house for party	☐ favors/party bags	2:30 _____
☐ decorate	☐	2:45 _____
☐	☐	3:00 _____
☐	☐	_____
☐ clean –up	☐	_____
☐ write thank you notes	☐	_____
☐ mail thank you notes	☐	_____
		_____

notes:	party info:
_____	date:_____
_____	time:_____
_____	theme:_____
_____	cake:_____
_____	favors: _____
_____	entertainment:

birthday party planner

to do:	to buy:	party schedule:
☐ select party date	☐ invitations	start _____
☐ make guest list	☐ stamps	0:15 _____
☐ address invitations	☐ paper cups	0:30 _____
☐ mail invitations	☐ paper plates	0:45 _____
☐ plan party theme	☐ napkins	1:00 _____
☐ decide on favors	☐ tablecloth	1:15 _____
☐ order birthday cake	☐ utensils	1:30 _____
☐ plan entertainment	☐ balloons	1:45 _____
☐ contact entertainers	☐ streamers/signs	2:00 _____
☐ buy food, décor items	☐ place cards	2:15 _____
☐ prepare house for party	☐ favors/party bags	2:30 _____
☐ decorate	☐	2:45 _____
☐	☐	3:00 _____
☐	☐	_____
☐ clean –up	☐	_____
☐ write thank you notes	☐	_____
☐ mail thank you notes	☐	_____

notes:	party info:
_____	date:_____
_____	time:_____
_____	theme:_____
_____	cake:_____
_____	favors: _____
_____	entertainment:

birthday party planner

to do:	to buy:	party schedule:
☐ select party date	☐ invitations	start _____
☐ make guest list	☐ stamps	0:15 _____
☐ address invitations	☐ paper cups	0:30 _____
☐ mail invitations	☐ paper plates	0:45 _____
☐ plan party theme	☐ napkins	1:00 _____
☐ decide on favors	☐ tablecloth	1:15 _____
☐ order birthday cake	☐ utensils	1:30 _____
☐ plan entertainment	☐ balloons	1:45 _____
☐ contact entertainers	☐ streamers/signs	2:00 _____
☐ buy food, décor items	☐ place cards	2:15 _____
☐ prepare house for party	☐ favors/party bags	2:30 _____
☐ decorate	☐	2:45 _____
☐	☐	3:00 _____
☐	☐	_____
☐ clean –up	☐	_____
☐ write thank you notes	☐	_____
☐ mail thank you notes	☐	_____

notes:	party info:
_____	date:_____
_____	time:_____
_____	theme:_____
_____	cake:_____
_____	favors: _____
_____	entertainment:

birthday party planner

to do:	to buy:	party schedule:
☐ select party date	☐ invitations	start _____
☐ make guest list	☐ stamps	0:15 _____
☐ address invitations	☐ paper cups	0:30 _____
☐ mail invitations	☐ paper plates	0:45 _____
☐ plan party theme	☐ napkins	1:00 _____
☐ decide on favors	☐ tablecloth	1:15 _____
☐ order birthday cake	☐ utensils	1:30 _____
☐ plan entertainment	☐ balloons	1:45 _____
☐ contact entertainers	☐ streamers/signs	2:00 _____
☐ buy food, décor items	☐ place cards	2:15 _____
☐ prepare house for party	☐ favors/party bags	2:30 _____
☐ decorate	☐	2:45 _____
☐	☐	3:00 _____
☐	☐	_____
☐ clean –up	☐	_____
☐ write thank you notes	☐	_____
☐ mail thank you notes	☐	_____

notes:	party info:
_____	date:_____
_____	time:_____
_____	theme:_____
_____	cake:_____
_____	favors: _____
_____	entertainment:

birthday party planner

to do:	to buy:	party schedule:
☐ select party date	☐ invitations	start _____
☐ make guest list	☐ stamps	0:15 _____
☐ address invitations	☐ paper cups	0:30 _____
☐ mail invitations	☐ paper plates	0:45 _____
☐ plan party theme	☐ napkins	1:00 _____
☐ decide on favors	☐ tablecloth	1:15 _____
☐ order birthday cake	☐ utensils	1:30 _____
☐ plan entertainment	☐ balloons	1:45 _____
☐ contact entertainers	☐ streamers/signs	2:00 _____
☐ buy food, décor items	☐ place cards	2:15 _____
☐ prepare house for party	☐ favors/party bags	2:30 _____
☐ decorate	☐	2:45 _____
☐	☐	3:00 _____
☐	☐	_____
☐ clean –up	☐	_____
☐ write thank you notes	☐	_____
☐ mail thank you notes	☐	_____

notes:	party info:
_____	date:_____
_____	time:_____
_____	theme:_____
_____	cake:_____
_____	favors: _____
_____	entertainment:

birthday party planner

to do:	to buy:	party schedule:
☐ select party date	☐ invitations	start _____
☐ make guest list	☐ stamps	0:15 _____
☐ address invitations	☐ paper cups	0:30 _____
☐ mail invitations	☐ paper plates	0:45 _____
☐ plan party theme	☐ napkins	1:00 _____
☐ decide on favors	☐ tablecloth	1:15 _____
☐ order birthday cake	☐ utensils	1:30 _____
☐ plan entertainment	☐ balloons	1:45 _____
☐ contact entertainers	☐ streamers/signs	2:00 _____
☐ buy food, décor items	☐ place cards	2:15 _____
☐ prepare house for party	☐ favors/party bags	2:30 _____
☐ decorate	☐	2:45 _____
☐	☐	3:00 _____
☐	☐	_____
☐ clean –up	☐	_____
☐ write thank you notes	☐	_____
☐ mail thank you notes	☐	_____

notes:	party info:
_____	date:_____
_____	time:_____
_____	theme:_____
_____	cake:_____
_____	favors: _____
_____	entertainment:

birthday party planner

to do:	to buy:	party schedule:
☐ select party date	☐ invitations	start _____
☐ make guest list	☐ stamps	0:15 _____
☐ address invitations	☐ paper cups	0:30 _____
☐ mail invitations	☐ paper plates	0:45 _____
☐ plan party theme	☐ napkins	1:00 _____
☐ decide on favors	☐ tablecloth	1:15 _____
☐ order birthday cake	☐ utensils	1:30 _____
☐ plan entertainment	☐ balloons	1:45 _____
☐ contact entertainers	☐ streamers/signs	2:00 _____
☐ buy food, décor items	☐ place cards	2:15 _____
☐ prepare house for party	☐ favors/party bags	2:30 _____
☐ decorate	☐	2:45 _____
☐	☐	3:00 _____
☐	☐	_____
☐ clean –up	☐	_____
☐ write thank you notes	☐	_____
☐ mail thank you notes	☐	_____
		_____

notes:	party info:
_____	date:_____
_____	time:_____
_____	theme:_____
_____	cake:_____
_____	favors: _____
_____	entertainment:

birthday party planner

to do:	to buy:	party schedule:
☐ select party date	☐ invitations	start _____
☐ make guest list	☐ stamps	0:15 _____
☐ address invitations	☐ paper cups	0:30 _____
☐ mail invitations	☐ paper plates	0:45 _____
☐ plan party theme	☐ napkins	1:00 _____
☐ decide on favors	☐ tablecloth	1:15 _____
☐ order birthday cake	☐ utensils	1:30 _____
☐ plan entertainment	☐ balloons	1:45 _____
☐ contact entertainers	☐ streamers/signs	2:00 _____
☐ buy food, décor items	☐ place cards	2:15 _____
☐ prepare house for party	☐ favors/party bags	2:30 _____
☐ decorate	☐	2:45 _____
☐	☐	3:00 _____
☐	☐	_____
☐ clean –up	☐	_____
☐ write thank you notes	☐	_____
☐ mail thank you notes	☐	_____

notes:	party info:
_____	date:_____
_____	time:_____
_____	theme:_____
_____	cake:_____
_____	favors: _____
_____	entertainment:

birthday party planner

to do:	to buy:	party schedule:
☐ select party date	☐ invitations	start _____
☐ make guest list	☐ stamps	0:15 _____
☐ address invitations	☐ paper cups	0:30 _____
☐ mail invitations	☐ paper plates	0:45 _____
☐ plan party theme	☐ napkins	1:00 _____
☐ decide on favors	☐ tablecloth	1:15 _____
☐ order birthday cake	☐ utensils	1:30 _____
☐ plan entertainment	☐ balloons	1:45 _____
☐ contact entertainers	☐ streamers/signs	2:00 _____
☐ buy food, décor items	☐ place cards	2:15 _____
☐ prepare house for party	☐ favors/party bags	2:30 _____
☐ decorate	☐	2:45 _____
☐	☐	3:00 _____
☐	☐	_____
☐ clean –up	☐	_____
☐ write thank you notes	☐	_____
☐ mail thank you notes	☐	_____

notes:	party info:
_____	date:_____
_____	time:_____
_____	theme:_____
_____	cake:_____
_____	favors: _____
_____	entertainment:

birthday party planner

to do:	to buy:	party schedule:
☐ select party date	☐ invitations	start _____
☐ make guest list	☐ stamps	0:15 _____
☐ address invitations	☐ paper cups	0:30 _____
☐ mail invitations	☐ paper plates	0:45 _____
☐ plan party theme	☐ napkins	1:00 _____
☐ decide on favors	☐ tablecloth	1:15 _____
☐ order birthday cake	☐ utensils	1:30 _____
☐ plan entertainment	☐ balloons	1:45 _____
☐ contact entertainers	☐ streamers/signs	2:00 _____
☐ buy food, décor items	☐ place cards	2:15 _____
☐ prepare house for party	☐ favors/party bags	2:30 _____
☐ decorate	☐	2:45 _____
☐	☐	3:00 _____
☐	☐	_____
☐ clean –up	☐	_____
☐ write thank you notes	☐	_____
☐ mail thank you notes	☐	_____

notes:	party info:
_____	date:_____
_____	time:_____
_____	theme:_____
_____	cake:_____
_____	favors: _____
_____	entertainment:

birthday party planner

to do:	to buy:	party schedule:
☐ select party date	☐ invitations	start _____
☐ make guest list	☐ stamps	0:15 _____
☐ address invitations	☐ paper cups	0:30 _____
☐ mail invitations	☐ paper plates	0:45 _____
☐ plan party theme	☐ napkins	1:00 _____
☐ decide on favors	☐ tablecloth	1:15 _____
☐ order birthday cake	☐ utensils	1:30 _____
☐ plan entertainment	☐ balloons	1:45 _____
☐ contact entertainers	☐ streamers/signs	2:00 _____
☐ buy food, décor items	☐ place cards	2:15 _____
☐ prepare house for party	☐ favors/party bags	2:30 _____
☐ decorate	☐	2:45 _____
☐	☐	3:00 _____
☐	☐	_____
☐ clean –up	☐	_____
☐ write thank you notes	☐	_____
☐ mail thank you notes	☐	_____

notes:	party info:
_____	date:_____
_____	time:_____
_____	theme:_____
_____	cake:_____
_____	favors: _____
_____	entertainment:

birthday party planner

to do:	to buy:	party schedule:
☐ select party date	☐ invitations	start _____
☐ make guest list	☐ stamps	0:15 _____
☐ address invitations	☐ paper cups	0:30 _____
☐ mail invitations	☐ paper plates	0:45 _____
☐ plan party theme	☐ napkins	1:00 _____
☐ decide on favors	☐ tablecloth	1:15 _____
☐ order birthday cake	☐ utensils	1:30 _____
☐ plan entertainment	☐ balloons	1:45 _____
☐ contact entertainers	☐ streamers/signs	2:00 _____
☐ buy food, décor items	☐ place cards	2:15 _____
☐ prepare house for party	☐ favors/party bags	2:30 _____
☐ decorate	☐	2:45 _____
☐	☐	3:00 _____
☐	☐	_____
☐ clean –up	☐	_____
☐ write thank you notes	☐	_____
☐ mail thank you notes	☐	_____

notes:	party info:
_____	date:_____
_____	time:_____
_____	theme:_____
_____	cake:_____
_____	favors: _____
_____	entertainment:

birthday party planner

to do:	to buy:	party schedule:
☐ select party date	☐ invitations	start _____
☐ make guest list	☐ stamps	0:15 _____
☐ address invitations	☐ paper cups	0:30 _____
☐ mail invitations	☐ paper plates	0:45 _____
☐ plan party theme	☐ napkins	1:00 _____
☐ decide on favors	☐ tablecloth	1:15 _____
☐ order birthday cake	☐ utensils	1:30 _____
☐ plan entertainment	☐ balloons	1:45 _____
☐ contact entertainers	☐ streamers/signs	2:00 _____
☐ buy food, décor items	☐ place cards	2:15 _____
☐ prepare house for party	☐ favors/party bags	2:30 _____
☐ decorate	☐	2:45 _____
☐	☐	3:00 _____
☐	☐	_____
☐ clean –up	☐	_____
☐ write thank you notes	☐	_____
☐ mail thank you notes	☐	_____

notes:	party info:
_____	date:_____
_____	time:_____
_____	theme:_____
_____	cake:_____
_____	favors: _____
_____	entertainment:

birthday party planner

to do:	to buy:	party schedule:
☐ select party date	☐ invitations	start _____
☐ make guest list	☐ stamps	0:15 _____
☐ address invitations	☐ paper cups	0:30 _____
☐ mail invitations	☐ paper plates	0:45 _____
☐ plan party theme	☐ napkins	1:00 _____
☐ decide on favors	☐ tablecloth	1:15 _____
☐ order birthday cake	☐ utensils	1:30 _____
☐ plan entertainment	☐ balloons	1:45 _____
☐ contact entertainers	☐ streamers/signs	2:00 _____
☐ buy food, décor items	☐ place cards	2:15 _____
☐ prepare house for party	☐ favors/party bags	2:30 _____
☐ decorate	☐	2:45 _____
☐	☐	3:00 _____
☐	☐	_____
☐ clean –up	☐	_____
☐ write thank you notes	☐	_____
☐ mail thank you notes	☐	_____

notes:	party info:
_____	date:_____
_____	time:_____
_____	theme:_____
_____	cake:_____
_____	favors: _____
_____	entertainment:

birthday party planner

to do:	to buy:	party schedule:
☐ select party date	☐ invitations	start _____
☐ make guest list	☐ stamps	0:15 _____
☐ address invitations	☐ paper cups	0:30 _____
☐ mail invitations	☐ paper plates	0:45 _____
☐ plan party theme	☐ napkins	1:00 _____
☐ decide on favors	☐ tablecloth	1:15 _____
☐ order birthday cake	☐ utensils	1:30 _____
☐ plan entertainment	☐ balloons	1:45 _____
☐ contact entertainers	☐ streamers/signs	2:00 _____
☐ buy food, décor items	☐ place cards	2:15 _____
☐ prepare house for party	☐ favors/party bags	2:30 _____
☐ decorate	☐	2:45 _____
☐	☐	3:00 _____
☐	☐	_____
☐ clean –up	☐	_____
☐ write thank you notes	☐	_____
☐ mail thank you notes	☐	_____

notes:	party info:
_____	date:_____
_____	time:_____
_____	theme:_____
_____	cake:_____
_____	favors: _____
_____	entertainment:

birthday party planner

to do:	to buy:	party schedule:
☐ select party date	☐ invitations	start _____
☐ make guest list	☐ stamps	0:15 _____
☐ address invitations	☐ paper cups	0:30 _____
☐ mail invitations	☐ paper plates	0:45 _____
☐ plan party theme	☐ napkins	1:00 _____
☐ decide on favors	☐ tablecloth	1:15 _____
☐ order birthday cake	☐ utensils	1:30 _____
☐ plan entertainment	☐ balloons	1:45 _____
☐ contact entertainers	☐ streamers/signs	2:00 _____
☐ buy food, décor items	☐ place cards	2:15 _____
☐ prepare house for party	☐ favors/party bags	2:30 _____
☐ decorate	☐	2:45 _____
☐	☐	3:00 _____
☐	☐	_____
☐ clean –up	☐	_____
☐ write thank you notes	☐	_____
☐ mail thank you notes	☐	_____

notes:	party info:
_____	date:_____
_____	time:_____
_____	theme:_____
_____	cake:_____
_____	favors: _____
_____	entertainment:

birthday party planner

to do:	to buy:	party schedule:
☐ select party date	☐ invitations	start _____
☐ make guest list	☐ stamps	0:15 _____
☐ address invitations	☐ paper cups	0:30 _____
☐ mail invitations	☐ paper plates	0:45 _____
☐ plan party theme	☐ napkins	1:00 _____
☐ decide on favors	☐ tablecloth	1:15 _____
☐ order birthday cake	☐ utensils	1:30 _____
☐ plan entertainment	☐ balloons	1:45 _____
☐ contact entertainers	☐ streamers/signs	2:00 _____
☐ buy food, décor items	☐ place cards	2:15 _____
☐ prepare house for party	☐ favors/party bags	2:30 _____
☐ decorate	☐	2:45 _____
☐	☐	3:00 _____
☐	☐	_____
☐ clean –up	☐	_____
☐ write thank you notes	☐	_____
☐ mail thank you notes	☐	_____

notes:	party info:
_____	date:_____
_____	time:_____
_____	theme:_____
_____	cake:_____
_____	favors: _____
_____	entertainment:

birthday party planner

to do:	to buy:	party schedule:
☐ select party date	☐ invitations	start _____
☐ make guest list	☐ stamps	0:15 _____
☐ address invitations	☐ paper cups	0:30 _____
☐ mail invitations	☐ paper plates	0:45 _____
☐ plan party theme	☐ napkins	1:00 _____
☐ decide on favors	☐ tablecloth	1:15 _____
☐ order birthday cake	☐ utensils	1:30 _____
☐ plan entertainment	☐ balloons	1:45 _____
☐ contact entertainers	☐ streamers/signs	2:00 _____
☐ buy food, décor items	☐ place cards	2:15 _____
☐ prepare house for party	☐ favors/party bags	2:30 _____
☐ decorate	☐	2:45 _____
☐	☐	3:00 _____
☐	☐	_____
☐ clean –up	☐	_____
☐ write thank you notes	☐	_____
☐ mail thank you notes	☐	_____

notes:	party info:
_____	date:_____
_____	time:_____
_____	theme:_____
_____	cake:_____
_____	favors: _____
_____	entertainment:

birthday party planner

to do:	to buy:	party schedule:
☐ select party date	☐ invitations	start _____
☐ make guest list	☐ stamps	0:15 _____
☐ address invitations	☐ paper cups	0:30 _____
☐ mail invitations	☐ paper plates	0:45 _____
☐ plan party theme	☐ napkins	1:00 _____
☐ decide on favors	☐ tablecloth	1:15 _____
☐ order birthday cake	☐ utensils	1:30 _____
☐ plan entertainment	☐ balloons	1:45 _____
☐ contact entertainers	☐ streamers/signs	2:00 _____
☐ buy food, décor items	☐ place cards	2:15 _____
☐ prepare house for party	☐ favors/party bags	2:30 _____
☐ decorate	☐	2:45 _____
☐	☐	3:00 _____
☐	☐	_____
☐ clean –up	☐	_____
☐ write thank you notes	☐	_____
☐ mail thank you notes	☐	_____

notes:	party info:
_____	date:_____
_____	time:_____
_____	theme:_____
_____	cake:_____
_____	favors: _____
_____	entertainment:

birthday party planner

to do:	to buy:	party schedule:
☐ select party date	☐ invitations	start _____
☐ make guest list	☐ stamps	0:15 _____
☐ address invitations	☐ paper cups	0:30 _____
☐ mail invitations	☐ paper plates	0:45 _____
☐ plan party theme	☐ napkins	1:00 _____
☐ decide on favors	☐ tablecloth	1:15 _____
☐ order birthday cake	☐ utensils	1:30 _____
☐ plan entertainment	☐ balloons	1:45 _____
☐ contact entertainers	☐ streamers/signs	2:00 _____
☐ buy food, décor items	☐ place cards	2:15 _____
☐ prepare house for party	☐ favors/party bags	2:30 _____
☐ decorate	☐	2:45 _____
☐	☐	3:00 _____
☐	☐	_____
☐ clean –up	☐	_____
☐ write thank you notes	☐	_____
☐ mail thank you notes	☐	_____

notes:	party info:
_____	date:_____
_____	time:_____
_____	theme:_____
_____	cake:_____
_____	favors: _____
_____	entertainment:

birthday party planner

to do:	to buy:	party schedule:
☐ select party date	☐ invitations	start _____
☐ make guest list	☐ stamps	0:15 _____
☐ address invitations	☐ paper cups	0:30 _____
☐ mail invitations	☐ paper plates	0:45 _____
☐ plan party theme	☐ napkins	1:00 _____
☐ decide on favors	☐ tablecloth	1:15 _____
☐ order birthday cake	☐ utensils	1:30 _____
☐ plan entertainment	☐ balloons	1:45 _____
☐ contact entertainers	☐ streamers/signs	2:00 _____
☐ buy food, décor items	☐ place cards	2:15 _____
☐ prepare house for party	☐ favors/party bags	2:30 _____
☐ decorate	☐	2:45 _____
☐	☐	3:00 _____
☐	☐	_____
☐ clean –up	☐	_____
☐ write thank you notes	☐	_____
☐ mail thank you notes	☐	_____

notes:	party info:
_____	date:_____
_____	time:_____
_____	theme:_____
_____	cake:_____
_____	favors: _____
_____	entertainment:

birthday party planner

to do:	to buy:	party schedule:
☐ select party date	☐ invitations	start _____
☐ make guest list	☐ stamps	0:15 _____
☐ address invitations	☐ paper cups	0:30 _____
☐ mail invitations	☐ paper plates	0:45 _____
☐ plan party theme	☐ napkins	1:00 _____
☐ decide on favors	☐ tablecloth	1:15 _____
☐ order birthday cake	☐ utensils	1:30 _____
☐ plan entertainment	☐ balloons	1:45 _____
☐ contact entertainers	☐ streamers/signs	2:00 _____
☐ buy food, décor items	☐ place cards	2:15 _____
☐ prepare house for party	☐ favors/party bags	2:30 _____
☐ decorate	☐	2:45 _____
☐	☐	3:00 _____
☐	☐	_____
☐ clean –up	☐	_____
☐ write thank you notes	☐	_____
☐ mail thank you notes	☐	_____

notes:	party info:
_____	date:_____
_____	time:_____
_____	theme:_____
_____	cake:_____
_____	favors: _____
_____	entertainment:

birthday party planner

to do:	to buy:	party schedule:
☐ select party date	☐ invitations	start _____
☐ make guest list	☐ stamps	0:15 _____
☐ address invitations	☐ paper cups	0:30 _____
☐ mail invitations	☐ paper plates	0:45 _____
☐ plan party theme	☐ napkins	1:00 _____
☐ decide on favors	☐ tablecloth	1:15 _____
☐ order birthday cake	☐ utensils	1:30 _____
☐ plan entertainment	☐ balloons	1:45 _____
☐ contact entertainers	☐ streamers/signs	2:00 _____
☐ buy food, décor items	☐ place cards	2:15 _____
☐ prepare house for party	☐ favors/party bags	2:30 _____
☐ decorate	☐	2:45 _____
☐	☐	3:00 _____
☐	☐	_____
☐ clean –up	☐	_____
☐ write thank you notes	☐	_____
☐ mail thank you notes	☐	_____

notes:	party info:
_____	date:_____
_____	time:_____
_____	theme:_____
_____	cake:_____
_____	favors: _____
_____	entertainment:

birthday party planner

to do:	to buy:	party schedule:
☐ select party date	☐ invitations	start _____
☐ make guest list	☐ stamps	0:15 _____
☐ address invitations	☐ paper cups	0:30 _____
☐ mail invitations	☐ paper plates	0:45 _____
☐ plan party theme	☐ napkins	1:00 _____
☐ decide on favors	☐ tablecloth	1:15 _____
☐ order birthday cake	☐ utensils	1:30 _____
☐ plan entertainment	☐ balloons	1:45 _____
☐ contact entertainers	☐ streamers/signs	2:00 _____
☐ buy food, décor items	☐ place cards	2:15 _____
☐ prepare house for party	☐ favors/party bags	2:30 _____
☐ decorate	☐	2:45 _____
☐	☐	3:00 _____
☐	☐	_____
☐ clean –up	☐	_____
☐ write thank you notes	☐	_____
☐ mail thank you notes	☐	_____

notes:	party info:
_____	date:_____
_____	time:_____
_____	theme:_____
_____	cake:_____
_____	favors: _____
_____	entertainment:

birthday party planner

to do:	to buy:	party schedule:
☐ select party date	☐ invitations	start _____
☐ make guest list	☐ stamps	0:15 _____
☐ address invitations	☐ paper cups	0:30 _____
☐ mail invitations	☐ paper plates	0:45 _____
☐ plan party theme	☐ napkins	1:00 _____
☐ decide on favors	☐ tablecloth	1:15 _____
☐ order birthday cake	☐ utensils	1:30 _____
☐ plan entertainment	☐ balloons	1:45 _____
☐ contact entertainers	☐ streamers/signs	2:00 _____
☐ buy food, décor items	☐ place cards	2:15 _____
☐ prepare house for party	☐ favors/party bags	2:30 _____
☐ decorate	☐	2:45 _____
☐	☐	3:00 _____
☐	☐	_____
☐ clean –up	☐	_____
☐ write thank you notes	☐	_____
☐ mail thank you notes	☐	_____

notes:	party info:
_____	date:_____
_____	time:_____
_____	theme:_____
_____	cake:_____
_____	favors: _____
_____	entertainment:

birthday party planner

to do:	to buy:	party schedule:
☐ select party date	☐ invitations	start _____
☐ make guest list	☐ stamps	0:15 _____
☐ address invitations	☐ paper cups	0:30 _____
☐ mail invitations	☐ paper plates	0:45 _____
☐ plan party theme	☐ napkins	1:00 _____
☐ decide on favors	☐ tablecloth	1:15 _____
☐ order birthday cake	☐ utensils	1:30 _____
☐ plan entertainment	☐ balloons	1:45 _____
☐ contact entertainers	☐ streamers/signs	2:00 _____
☐ buy food, décor items	☐ place cards	2:15 _____
☐ prepare house for party	☐ favors/party bags	2:30 _____
☐ decorate	☐	2:45 _____
☐	☐	3:00 _____
☐	☐	_____
☐ clean –up	☐	_____
☐ write thank you notes	☐	_____
☐ mail thank you notes	☐	_____

notes:	party info:
_____	date:_____
_____	time:_____
_____	theme:_____
_____	cake:_____
_____	favors: _____
_____	entertainment:

birthday party planner

to do:	to buy:	party schedule:
☐ select party date	☐ invitations	start _____
☐ make guest list	☐ stamps	0:15 _____
☐ address invitations	☐ paper cups	0:30 _____
☐ mail invitations	☐ paper plates	0:45 _____
☐ plan party theme	☐ napkins	1:00 _____
☐ decide on favors	☐ tablecloth	1:15 _____
☐ order birthday cake	☐ utensils	1:30 _____
☐ plan entertainment	☐ balloons	1:45 _____
☐ contact entertainers	☐ streamers/signs	2:00 _____
☐ buy food, décor items	☐ place cards	2:15 _____
☐ prepare house for party	☐ favors/party bags	2:30 _____
☐ decorate	☐	2:45 _____
☐	☐	3:00 _____
☐	☐	_____
☐ clean –up	☐	_____
☐ write thank you notes	☐	_____
☐ mail thank you notes	☐	_____

notes:	party info:
_____	date:_____
_____	time:_____
_____	theme:_____
_____	cake:_____
_____	favors: _____
_____	entertainment:

birthday party planner

to do:	to buy:	party schedule:
☐ select party date	☐ invitations	start _____
☐ make guest list	☐ stamps	0:15 _____
☐ address invitations	☐ paper cups	0:30 _____
☐ mail invitations	☐ paper plates	0:45 _____
☐ plan party theme	☐ napkins	1:00 _____
☐ decide on favors	☐ tablecloth	1:15 _____
☐ order birthday cake	☐ utensils	1:30 _____
☐ plan entertainment	☐ balloons	1:45 _____
☐ contact entertainers	☐ streamers/signs	2:00 _____
☐ buy food, décor items	☐ place cards	2:15 _____
☐ prepare house for party	☐ favors/party bags	2:30 _____
☐ decorate	☐	2:45 _____
☐	☐	3:00 _____
☐	☐	_____
☐ clean –up	☐	_____
☐ write thank you notes	☐	_____
☐ mail thank you notes	☐	_____

notes:	party info:
_____	date:_____
_____	time:_____
_____	theme:_____
_____	cake:_____
_____	favors: _____
_____	entertainment:

birthday party planner

to do:	to buy:	party schedule:
☐ select party date	☐ invitations	start _____
☐ make guest list	☐ stamps	0:15 _____
☐ address invitations	☐ paper cups	0:30 _____
☐ mail invitations	☐ paper plates	0:45 _____
☐ plan party theme	☐ napkins	1:00 _____
☐ decide on favors	☐ tablecloth	1:15 _____
☐ order birthday cake	☐ utensils	1:30 _____
☐ plan entertainment	☐ balloons	1:45 _____
☐ contact entertainers	☐ streamers/signs	2:00 _____
☐ buy food, décor items	☐ place cards	2:15 _____
☐ prepare house for party	☐ favors/party bags	2:30 _____
☐ decorate	☐	2:45 _____
☐	☐	3:00 _____
☐	☐	_____
☐ clean –up	☐	_____
☐ write thank you notes	☐	_____
☐ mail thank you notes	☐	_____

notes:	party info:
_____	date:_____
_____	time:_____
_____	theme:_____
_____	cake:_____
_____	favors: _____
_____	entertainment:

birthday party planner

to do:	to buy:	party schedule:
☐ select party date	☐ invitations	start _____
☐ make guest list	☐ stamps	0:15 _____
☐ address invitations	☐ paper cups	0:30 _____
☐ mail invitations	☐ paper plates	0:45 _____
☐ plan party theme	☐ napkins	1:00 _____
☐ decide on favors	☐ tablecloth	1:15 _____
☐ order birthday cake	☐ utensils	1:30 _____
☐ plan entertainment	☐ balloons	1:45 _____
☐ contact entertainers	☐ streamers/signs	2:00 _____
☐ buy food, décor items	☐ place cards	2:15 _____
☐ prepare house for party	☐ favors/party bags	2:30 _____
☐ decorate	☐	2:45 _____
☐	☐	3:00 _____
☐	☐	_____
☐ clean –up	☐	_____
☐ write thank you notes	☐	_____
☐ mail thank you notes	☐	_____

notes:	party info:
_____	date:_____
_____	time:_____
_____	theme:_____
_____	cake:_____
_____	favors: _____
_____	entertainment:

birthday party planner

to do:	to buy:	party schedule:
☐ select party date	☐ invitations	start _____
☐ make guest list	☐ stamps	0:15 _____
☐ address invitations	☐ paper cups	0:30 _____
☐ mail invitations	☐ paper plates	0:45 _____
☐ plan party theme	☐ napkins	1:00 _____
☐ decide on favors	☐ tablecloth	1:15 _____
☐ order birthday cake	☐ utensils	1:30 _____
☐ plan entertainment	☐ balloons	1:45 _____
☐ contact entertainers	☐ streamers/signs	2:00 _____
☐ buy food, décor items	☐ place cards	2:15 _____
☐ prepare house for party	☐ favors/party bags	2:30 _____
☐ decorate	☐	2:45 _____
☐	☐	3:00 _____
☐	☐	_____
☐ clean –up	☐	_____
☐ write thank you notes	☐	_____
☐ mail thank you notes	☐	_____

notes:	party info:
_____	date:_____
_____	time:_____
_____	theme:_____
_____	cake:_____
_____	favors: _____
_____	entertainment:

birthday party planner

to do:	to buy:	party schedule:
☐ select party date	☐ invitations	start _____
☐ make guest list	☐ stamps	0:15 _____
☐ address invitations	☐ paper cups	0:30 _____
☐ mail invitations	☐ paper plates	0:45 _____
☐ plan party theme	☐ napkins	1:00 _____
☐ decide on favors	☐ tablecloth	1:15 _____
☐ order birthday cake	☐ utensils	1:30 _____
☐ plan entertainment	☐ balloons	1:45 _____
☐ contact entertainers	☐ streamers/signs	2:00 _____
☐ buy food, décor items	☐ place cards	2:15 _____
☐ prepare house for party	☐ favors/party bags	2:30 _____
☐ decorate	☐	2:45 _____
☐	☐	3:00 _____
☐	☐	_____
☐ clean –up	☐	_____
☐ write thank you notes	☐	_____
☐ mail thank you notes	☐	_____

notes:	party info:
_____	date:_____
_____	time:_____
_____	theme:_____
_____	cake:_____
_____	favors: _____
_____	entertainment:

birthday party planner

to do:	to buy:	party schedule:
☐ select party date	☐ invitations	start _____
☐ make guest list	☐ stamps	0:15 _____
☐ address invitations	☐ paper cups	0:30 _____
☐ mail invitations	☐ paper plates	0:45 _____
☐ plan party theme	☐ napkins	1:00 _____
☐ decide on favors	☐ tablecloth	1:15 _____
☐ order birthday cake	☐ utensils	1:30 _____
☐ plan entertainment	☐ balloons	1:45 _____
☐ contact entertainers	☐ streamers/signs	2:00 _____
☐ buy food, décor items	☐ place cards	2:15 _____
☐ prepare house for party	☐ favors/party bags	2:30 _____
☐ decorate	☐	2:45 _____
☐	☐	3:00 _____
☐	☐	_____
☐ clean –up	☐	_____
☐ write thank you notes	☐	_____
☐ mail thank you notes	☐	_____

notes:	party info:
_____	date:_____
_____	time:_____
_____	theme:_____
_____	cake:_____
_____	favors: _____
_____	entertainment:

birthday party planner

to do:	to buy:	party schedule:
☐ select party date	☐ invitations	start _____
☐ make guest list	☐ stamps	0:15 _____
☐ address invitations	☐ paper cups	0:30 _____
☐ mail invitations	☐ paper plates	0:45 _____
☐ plan party theme	☐ napkins	1:00 _____
☐ decide on favors	☐ tablecloth	1:15 _____
☐ order birthday cake	☐ utensils	1:30 _____
☐ plan entertainment	☐ balloons	1:45 _____
☐ contact entertainers	☐ streamers/signs	2:00 _____
☐ buy food, décor items	☐ place cards	2:15 _____
☐ prepare house for party	☐ favors/party bags	2:30 _____
☐ decorate	☐	2:45 _____
☐	☐	3:00 _____
☐	☐	_____
☐ clean –up	☐	_____
☐ write thank you notes	☐	_____
☐ mail thank you notes	☐	_____

notes:	party info:
_____	date:_____
_____	time:_____
_____	theme:_____
_____	cake:_____
_____	favors: _____
_____	entertainment:

birthday party planner

to do:	to buy:	party schedule:
☐ select party date	☐ invitations	start _____
☐ make guest list	☐ stamps	0:15 _____
☐ address invitations	☐ paper cups	0:30 _____
☐ mail invitations	☐ paper plates	0:45 _____
☐ plan party theme	☐ napkins	1:00 _____
☐ decide on favors	☐ tablecloth	1:15 _____
☐ order birthday cake	☐ utensils	1:30 _____
☐ plan entertainment	☐ balloons	1:45 _____
☐ contact entertainers	☐ streamers/signs	2:00 _____
☐ buy food, décor items	☐ place cards	2:15 _____
☐ prepare house for party	☐ favors/party bags	2:30 _____
☐ decorate	☐	2:45 _____
☐	☐	3:00 _____
☐	☐	_____
☐ clean –up	☐	_____
☐ write thank you notes	☐	_____
☐ mail thank you notes	☐	_____

notes:	party info:
_____	date:_____
_____	time:_____
_____	theme:_____
_____	cake:_____
_____	favors: _____
_____	entertainment:

birthday party planner

to do:	to buy:	party schedule:
☐ select party date	☐ invitations	start _____
☐ make guest list	☐ stamps	0:15 _____
☐ address invitations	☐ paper cups	0:30 _____
☐ mail invitations	☐ paper plates	0:45 _____
☐ plan party theme	☐ napkins	1:00 _____
☐ decide on favors	☐ tablecloth	1:15 _____
☐ order birthday cake	☐ utensils	1:30 _____
☐ plan entertainment	☐ balloons	1:45 _____
☐ contact entertainers	☐ streamers/signs	2:00 _____
☐ buy food, décor items	☐ place cards	2:15 _____
☐ prepare house for party	☐ favors/party bags	2:30 _____
☐ decorate	☐	2:45 _____
☐	☐	3:00 _____
☐	☐	_____
☐ clean –up	☐	_____
☐ write thank you notes	☐	_____
☐ mail thank you notes	☐	_____

notes:	party info:
_____	date:_____
_____	time:_____
_____	theme:_____
_____	cake:_____
_____	favors: _____
_____	entertainment:

birthday party planner

to do:	to buy:	party schedule:
☐ select party date	☐ invitations	start _____
☐ make guest list	☐ stamps	0:15 _____
☐ address invitations	☐ paper cups	0:30 _____
☐ mail invitations	☐ paper plates	0:45 _____
☐ plan party theme	☐ napkins	1:00 _____
☐ decide on favors	☐ tablecloth	1:15 _____
☐ order birthday cake	☐ utensils	1:30 _____
☐ plan entertainment	☐ balloons	1:45 _____
☐ contact entertainers	☐ streamers/signs	2:00 _____
☐ buy food, décor items	☐ place cards	2:15 _____
☐ prepare house for party	☐ favors/party bags	2:30 _____
☐ decorate	☐	2:45 _____
☐	☐	3:00 _____
☐	☐	_____
☐ clean –up	☐	_____
☐ write thank you notes	☐	_____
☐ mail thank you notes	☐	_____

notes:	party info:
_____	date:_____
_____	time:_____
_____	theme:_____
_____	cake:_____
_____	favors: _____
_____	entertainment:

birthday party planner

to do:	to buy:	party schedule:
☐ select party date	☐ invitations	start _____
☐ make guest list	☐ stamps	0:15 _____
☐ address invitations	☐ paper cups	0:30 _____
☐ mail invitations	☐ paper plates	0:45 _____
☐ plan party theme	☐ napkins	1:00 _____
☐ decide on favors	☐ tablecloth	1:15 _____
☐ order birthday cake	☐ utensils	1:30 _____
☐ plan entertainment	☐ balloons	1:45 _____
☐ contact entertainers	☐ streamers/signs	2:00 _____
☐ buy food, décor items	☐ place cards	2:15 _____
☐ prepare house for party	☐ favors/party bags	2:30 _____
☐ decorate	☐	2:45 _____
☐	☐	3:00 _____
☐	☐	_____
☐ clean –up	☐	_____
☐ write thank you notes	☐	_____
☐ mail thank you notes	☐	_____

notes:	party info:
_____	date:_____
_____	time:_____
_____	theme:_____
_____	cake:_____
_____	favors: _____
_____	entertainment:

birthday party planner

to do:	to buy:	party schedule:
☐ select party date	☐ invitations	start _____
☐ make guest list	☐ stamps	0:15 _____
☐ address invitations	☐ paper cups	0:30 _____
☐ mail invitations	☐ paper plates	0:45 _____
☐ plan party theme	☐ napkins	1:00 _____
☐ decide on favors	☐ tablecloth	1:15 _____
☐ order birthday cake	☐ utensils	1:30 _____
☐ plan entertainment	☐ balloons	1:45 _____
☐ contact entertainers	☐ streamers/signs	2:00 _____
☐ buy food, décor items	☐ place cards	2:15 _____
☐ prepare house for party	☐ favors/party bags	2:30 _____
☐ decorate	☐	2:45 _____
☐	☐	3:00 _____
☐	☐	_____
☐ clean –up	☐	_____
☐ write thank you notes	☐	_____
☐ mail thank you notes	☐	_____

notes:	party info:
_____	date:_____
_____	time:_____
_____	theme:_____
_____	cake:_____
_____	favors: _____
_____	entertainment:

birthday party planner

to do:	to buy:	party schedule:
☐ select party date	☐ invitations	start _____
☐ make guest list	☐ stamps	0:15 _____
☐ address invitations	☐ paper cups	0:30 _____
☐ mail invitations	☐ paper plates	0:45 _____
☐ plan party theme	☐ napkins	1:00 _____
☐ decide on favors	☐ tablecloth	1:15 _____
☐ order birthday cake	☐ utensils	1:30 _____
☐ plan entertainment	☐ balloons	1:45 _____
☐ contact entertainers	☐ streamers/signs	2:00 _____
☐ buy food, décor items	☐ place cards	2:15 _____
☐ prepare house for party	☐ favors/party bags	2:30 _____
☐ decorate	☐	2:45 _____
☐	☐	3:00 _____
☐	☐	_____
☐ clean –up	☐	_____
☐ write thank you notes	☐	_____
☐ mail thank you notes	☐	_____

notes:	party info:
_____	date:_____
_____	time:_____
_____	theme:_____
_____	cake:_____
_____	favors: _____
_____	entertainment:

birthday party planner

to do:	to buy:	party schedule:
☐ select party date	☐ invitations	start _____
☐ make guest list	☐ stamps	0:15 _____
☐ address invitations	☐ paper cups	0:30 _____
☐ mail invitations	☐ paper plates	0:45 _____
☐ plan party theme	☐ napkins	1:00 _____
☐ decide on favors	☐ tablecloth	1:15 _____
☐ order birthday cake	☐ utensils	1:30 _____
☐ plan entertainment	☐ balloons	1:45 _____
☐ contact entertainers	☐ streamers/signs	2:00 _____
☐ buy food, décor items	☐ place cards	2:15 _____
☐ prepare house for party	☐ favors/party bags	2:30 _____
☐ decorate	☐	2:45 _____
☐	☐	3:00 _____
☐	☐	_____
☐ clean –up	☐	_____
☐ write thank you notes	☐	_____
☐ mail thank you notes	☐	_____

notes:	party info:
_____	date:_____
_____	time:_____
_____	theme:_____
_____	cake:_____
_____	favors: _____
_____	entertainment:

birthday party planner

to do:	to buy:	party schedule:
☐ select party date	☐ invitations	start _____
☐ make guest list	☐ stamps	0:15 _____
☐ address invitations	☐ paper cups	0:30 _____
☐ mail invitations	☐ paper plates	0:45 _____
☐ plan party theme	☐ napkins	1:00 _____
☐ decide on favors	☐ tablecloth	1:15 _____
☐ order birthday cake	☐ utensils	1:30 _____
☐ plan entertainment	☐ balloons	1:45 _____
☐ contact entertainers	☐ streamers/signs	2:00 _____
☐ buy food, décor items	☐ place cards	2:15 _____
☐ prepare house for party	☐ favors/party bags	2:30 _____
☐ decorate	☐	2:45 _____
☐	☐	3:00 _____
☐	☐	_____
☐ clean –up	☐	_____
☐ write thank you notes	☐	_____
☐ mail thank you notes	☐	_____

notes:	party info:
_____	date:_____
_____	time:_____
_____	theme:_____
_____	cake:_____
_____	favors: _____
_____	entertainment:

birthday party planner

to do:	to buy:	party schedule:
☐ select party date	☐ invitations	start _____
☐ make guest list	☐ stamps	0:15 _____
☐ address invitations	☐ paper cups	0:30 _____
☐ mail invitations	☐ paper plates	0:45 _____
☐ plan party theme	☐ napkins	1:00 _____
☐ decide on favors	☐ tablecloth	1:15 _____
☐ order birthday cake	☐ utensils	1:30 _____
☐ plan entertainment	☐ balloons	1:45 _____
☐ contact entertainers	☐ streamers/signs	2:00 _____
☐ buy food, décor items	☐ place cards	2:15 _____
☐ prepare house for party	☐ favors/party bags	2:30 _____
☐ decorate	☐	2:45 _____
☐	☐	3:00 _____
☐	☐	_____
☐ clean –up	☐	_____
☐ write thank you notes	☐	_____
☐ mail thank you notes	☐	_____

notes:	party info:
_____	date:_____
_____	time:_____
_____	theme:_____
_____	cake:_____
_____	favors: _____
_____	entertainment:

birthday party planner

to do:	to buy:	party schedule:
☐ select party date	☐ invitations	start _____
☐ make guest list	☐ stamps	0:15 _____
☐ address invitations	☐ paper cups	0:30 _____
☐ mail invitations	☐ paper plates	0:45 _____
☐ plan party theme	☐ napkins	1:00 _____
☐ decide on favors	☐ tablecloth	1:15 _____
☐ order birthday cake	☐ utensils	1:30 _____
☐ plan entertainment	☐ balloons	1:45 _____
☐ contact entertainers	☐ streamers/signs	2:00 _____
☐ buy food, décor items	☐ place cards	2:15 _____
☐ prepare house for party	☐ favors/party bags	2:30 _____
☐ decorate	☐	2:45 _____
☐	☐	3:00 _____
☐	☐	_____
☐ clean –up	☐	_____
☐ write thank you notes	☐	_____
☐ mail thank you notes	☐	_____

notes:	party info:
_____	date:_____
_____	time:_____
_____	theme:_____
_____	cake:_____
_____	favors: _____
_____	entertainment:

birthday party planner

to do:	to buy:	party schedule:
☐ select party date	☐ invitations	start _____
☐ make guest list	☐ stamps	0:15 _____
☐ address invitations	☐ paper cups	0:30 _____
☐ mail invitations	☐ paper plates	0:45 _____
☐ plan party theme	☐ napkins	1:00 _____
☐ decide on favors	☐ tablecloth	1:15 _____
☐ order birthday cake	☐ utensils	1:30 _____
☐ plan entertainment	☐ balloons	1:45 _____
☐ contact entertainers	☐ streamers/signs	2:00 _____
☐ buy food, décor items	☐ place cards	2:15 _____
☐ prepare house for party	☐ favors/party bags	2:30 _____
☐ decorate	☐	2:45 _____
☐	☐	3:00 _____
☐	☐	_____
☐ clean –up	☐	_____
☐ write thank you notes	☐	_____
☐ mail thank you notes	☐	_____

notes:	party info:
_____	date:_____
_____	time:_____
_____	theme:_____
_____	cake:_____
_____	favors: _____
_____	entertainment:

birthday party planner

to do:	to buy:	party schedule:
☐ select party date	☐ invitations	start _____
☐ make guest list	☐ stamps	0:15 _____
☐ address invitations	☐ paper cups	0:30 _____
☐ mail invitations	☐ paper plates	0:45 _____
☐ plan party theme	☐ napkins	1:00 _____
☐ decide on favors	☐ tablecloth	1:15 _____
☐ order birthday cake	☐ utensils	1:30 _____
☐ plan entertainment	☐ balloons	1:45 _____
☐ contact entertainers	☐ streamers/signs	2:00 _____
☐ buy food, décor items	☐ place cards	2:15 _____
☐ prepare house for party	☐ favors/party bags	2:30 _____
☐ decorate	☐	2:45 _____
☐	☐	3:00 _____
☐	☐	_____
☐ clean –up	☐	_____
☐ write thank you notes	☐	_____
☐ mail thank you notes	☐	_____

notes:	party info:
_____	date:_____
_____	time:_____
_____	theme:_____
_____	cake:_____
_____	favors: _____
_____	entertainment:

birthday party planner

to do:	to buy:	party schedule:
☐ select party date	☐ invitations	start _____
☐ make guest list	☐ stamps	0:15 _____
☐ address invitations	☐ paper cups	0:30 _____
☐ mail invitations	☐ paper plates	0:45 _____
☐ plan party theme	☐ napkins	1:00 _____
☐ decide on favors	☐ tablecloth	1:15 _____
☐ order birthday cake	☐ utensils	1:30 _____
☐ plan entertainment	☐ balloons	1:45 _____
☐ contact entertainers	☐ streamers/signs	2:00 _____
☐ buy food, décor items	☐ place cards	2:15 _____
☐ prepare house for party	☐ favors/party bags	2:30 _____
☐ decorate	☐	2:45 _____
☐	☐	3:00 _____
☐	☐	_____
☐ clean –up	☐	_____
☐ write thank you notes	☐	_____
☐ mail thank you notes	☐	_____
		_____

notes:	party info:
_____	date:_____
_____	time:_____
_____	theme:_____
_____	cake:_____
_____	favors: _____
_____	entertainment:

birthday party planner

to do:	to buy:	party schedule:
☐ select party date	☐ invitations	start _____
☐ make guest list	☐ stamps	0:15 _____
☐ address invitations	☐ paper cups	0:30 _____
☐ mail invitations	☐ paper plates	0:45 _____
☐ plan party theme	☐ napkins	1:00 _____
☐ decide on favors	☐ tablecloth	1:15 _____
☐ order birthday cake	☐ utensils	1:30 _____
☐ plan entertainment	☐ balloons	1:45 _____
☐ contact entertainers	☐ streamers/signs	2:00 _____
☐ buy food, décor items	☐ place cards	2:15 _____
☐ prepare house for party	☐ favors/party bags	2:30 _____
☐ decorate	☐	2:45 _____
☐	☐	3:00 _____
☐	☐	_____
☐ clean –up	☐	_____
☐ write thank you notes	☐	_____
☐ mail thank you notes	☐	_____

notes:	party info:
_____	date:_____
_____	time:_____
_____	theme:_____
_____	cake:_____
_____	favors: _____
_____	entertainment:

birthday party planner

to do:	to buy:	party schedule:
☐ select party date	☐ invitations	start _____
☐ make guest list	☐ stamps	0:15 _____
☐ address invitations	☐ paper cups	0:30 _____
☐ mail invitations	☐ paper plates	0:45 _____
☐ plan party theme	☐ napkins	1:00 _____
☐ decide on favors	☐ tablecloth	1:15 _____
☐ order birthday cake	☐ utensils	1:30 _____
☐ plan entertainment	☐ balloons	1:45 _____
☐ contact entertainers	☐ streamers/signs	2:00 _____
☐ buy food, décor items	☐ place cards	2:15 _____
☐ prepare house for party	☐ favors/party bags	2:30 _____
☐ decorate	☐	2:45 _____
☐	☐	3:00 _____
☐	☐	_____
☐ clean –up	☐	_____
☐ write thank you notes	☐	_____
☐ mail thank you notes	☐	_____

notes:	party info:
_____	date:_____
_____	time:_____
_____	theme:_____
_____	cake:_____
_____	favors: _____
_____	entertainment:

birthday party planner

to do:	to buy:	party schedule:
☐ select party date	☐ invitations	start _____
☐ make guest list	☐ stamps	0:15 _____
☐ address invitations	☐ paper cups	0:30 _____
☐ mail invitations	☐ paper plates	0:45 _____
☐ plan party theme	☐ napkins	1:00 _____
☐ decide on favors	☐ tablecloth	1:15 _____
☐ order birthday cake	☐ utensils	1:30 _____
☐ plan entertainment	☐ balloons	1:45 _____
☐ contact entertainers	☐ streamers/signs	2:00 _____
☐ buy food, décor items	☐ place cards	2:15 _____
☐ prepare house for party	☐ favors/party bags	2:30 _____
☐ decorate	☐	2:45 _____
☐	☐	3:00 _____
☐	☐	_____
☐ clean –up	☐	_____
☐ write thank you notes	☐	_____
☐ mail thank you notes	☐	_____

notes:	party info:
_____	date:_____
_____	time:_____
_____	theme:_____
_____	cake:_____
_____	favors: _____
_____	entertainment:

birthday party planner

to do:	to buy:	party schedule:
☐ select party date	☐ invitations	start _____
☐ make guest list	☐ stamps	0:15 _____
☐ address invitations	☐ paper cups	0:30 _____
☐ mail invitations	☐ paper plates	0:45 _____
☐ plan party theme	☐ napkins	1:00 _____
☐ decide on favors	☐ tablecloth	1:15 _____
☐ order birthday cake	☐ utensils	1:30 _____
☐ plan entertainment	☐ balloons	1:45 _____
☐ contact entertainers	☐ streamers/signs	2:00 _____
☐ buy food, décor items	☐ place cards	2:15 _____
☐ prepare house for party	☐ favors/party bags	2:30 _____
☐ decorate	☐	2:45 _____
☐	☐	3:00 _____
☐	☐	_____
☐ clean –up	☐	_____
☐ write thank you notes	☐	_____
☐ mail thank you notes	☐	_____

notes:	party info:
_____	date:_____
_____	time:_____
_____	theme:_____
_____	cake:_____
_____	favors: _____
_____	entertainment:

birthday party planner

to do:	to buy:	party schedule:
☐ select party date	☐ invitations	start _____
☐ make guest list	☐ stamps	0:15 _____
☐ address invitations	☐ paper cups	0:30 _____
☐ mail invitations	☐ paper plates	0:45 _____
☐ plan party theme	☐ napkins	1:00 _____
☐ decide on favors	☐ tablecloth	1:15 _____
☐ order birthday cake	☐ utensils	1:30 _____
☐ plan entertainment	☐ balloons	1:45 _____
☐ contact entertainers	☐ streamers/signs	2:00 _____
☐ buy food, décor items	☐ place cards	2:15 _____
☐ prepare house for party	☐ favors/party bags	2:30 _____
☐ decorate	☐	2:45 _____
☐	☐	3:00 _____
☐	☐	_____
☐ clean –up	☐	_____
☐ write thank you notes	☐	_____
☐ mail thank you notes	☐	_____

notes:	party info:
_____	date:_____
_____	time:_____
_____	theme:_____
_____	cake:_____
_____	favors: _____
_____	entertainment:

birthday party planner

to do:	to buy:	party schedule:
☐ select party date	☐ invitations	start _____
☐ make guest list	☐ stamps	0:15 _____
☐ address invitations	☐ paper cups	0:30 _____
☐ mail invitations	☐ paper plates	0:45 _____
☐ plan party theme	☐ napkins	1:00 _____
☐ decide on favors	☐ tablecloth	1:15 _____
☐ order birthday cake	☐ utensils	1:30 _____
☐ plan entertainment	☐ balloons	1:45 _____
☐ contact entertainers	☐ streamers/signs	2:00 _____
☐ buy food, décor items	☐ place cards	2:15 _____
☐ prepare house for party	☐ favors/party bags	2:30 _____
☐ decorate	☐	2:45 _____
☐	☐	3:00 _____
☐	☐	_____
☐ clean –up	☐	_____
☐ write thank you notes	☐	_____
☐ mail thank you notes	☐	_____

notes:	party info:
_____	date:_____
_____	time:_____
_____	theme:_____
_____	cake:_____
_____	favors: _____
_____	entertainment:

birthday party planner

to do:	to buy:	party schedule:
☐ select party date	☐ invitations	start _____
☐ make guest list	☐ stamps	0:15 _____
☐ address invitations	☐ paper cups	0:30 _____
☐ mail invitations	☐ paper plates	0:45 _____
☐ plan party theme	☐ napkins	1:00 _____
☐ decide on favors	☐ tablecloth	1:15 _____
☐ order birthday cake	☐ utensils	1:30 _____
☐ plan entertainment	☐ balloons	1:45 _____
☐ contact entertainers	☐ streamers/signs	2:00 _____
☐ buy food, décor items	☐ place cards	2:15 _____
☐ prepare house for party	☐ favors/party bags	2:30 _____
☐ decorate	☐	2:45 _____
☐	☐	3:00 _____
☐	☐	_____
☐ clean –up	☐	_____
☐ write thank you notes	☐	_____
☐ mail thank you notes	☐	_____

notes:	party info:
_____	date:_____
_____	time:_____
_____	theme:_____
_____	cake:_____
_____	favors: _____
_____	entertainment:

birthday party planner

to do:	to buy:	party schedule:
☐ select party date	☐ invitations	start _____
☐ make guest list	☐ stamps	0:15 _____
☐ address invitations	☐ paper cups	0:30 _____
☐ mail invitations	☐ paper plates	0:45 _____
☐ plan party theme	☐ napkins	1:00 _____
☐ decide on favors	☐ tablecloth	1:15 _____
☐ order birthday cake	☐ utensils	1:30 _____
☐ plan entertainment	☐ balloons	1:45 _____
☐ contact entertainers	☐ streamers/signs	2:00 _____
☐ buy food, décor items	☐ place cards	2:15 _____
☐ prepare house for party	☐ favors/party bags	2:30 _____
☐ decorate	☐	2:45 _____
☐	☐	3:00 _____
☐	☐	_____
☐ clean –up	☐	_____
☐ write thank you notes	☐	_____
☐ mail thank you notes	☐	_____

notes:	party info:
_____	date:_____
_____	time:_____
_____	theme:_____
_____	cake:_____
_____	favors: _____
_____	entertainment:

birthday party planner

to do:	to buy:	party schedule:
☐ select party date	☐ invitations	start _____
☐ make guest list	☐ stamps	0:15 _____
☐ address invitations	☐ paper cups	0:30 _____
☐ mail invitations	☐ paper plates	0:45 _____
☐ plan party theme	☐ napkins	1:00 _____
☐ decide on favors	☐ tablecloth	1:15 _____
☐ order birthday cake	☐ utensils	1:30 _____
☐ plan entertainment	☐ balloons	1:45 _____
☐ contact entertainers	☐ streamers/signs	2:00 _____
☐ buy food, décor items	☐ place cards	2:15 _____
☐ prepare house for party	☐ favors/party bags	2:30 _____
☐ decorate	☐	2:45 _____
☐	☐	3:00 _____
☐	☐	_____
☐ clean –up	☐	_____
☐ write thank you notes	☐	_____
☐ mail thank you notes	☐	_____

notes:	party info:
_____	date:_____
_____	time:_____
_____	theme:_____
_____	cake:_____
_____	favors: _____
_____	entertainment:

birthday party planner

to do:	to buy:	party schedule:
☐ select party date	☐ invitations	start _____
☐ make guest list	☐ stamps	0:15 _____
☐ address invitations	☐ paper cups	0:30 _____
☐ mail invitations	☐ paper plates	0:45 _____
☐ plan party theme	☐ napkins	1:00 _____
☐ decide on favors	☐ tablecloth	1:15 _____
☐ order birthday cake	☐ utensils	1:30 _____
☐ plan entertainment	☐ balloons	1:45 _____
☐ contact entertainers	☐ streamers/signs	2:00 _____
☐ buy food, décor items	☐ place cards	2:15 _____
☐ prepare house for party	☐ favors/party bags	2:30 _____
☐ decorate	☐	2:45 _____
☐	☐	3:00 _____
☐	☐	_____
☐ clean –up	☐	_____
☐ write thank you notes	☐	_____
☐ mail thank you notes	☐	_____

notes:	party info:
_____	date:_____
_____	time:_____
_____	theme:_____
_____	cake:_____
_____	favors: _____
_____	entertainment:

birthday party planner

to do:	to buy:	party schedule:
☐ select party date	☐ invitations	start _____
☐ make guest list	☐ stamps	0:15 _____
☐ address invitations	☐ paper cups	0:30 _____
☐ mail invitations	☐ paper plates	0:45 _____
☐ plan party theme	☐ napkins	1:00 _____
☐ decide on favors	☐ tablecloth	1:15 _____
☐ order birthday cake	☐ utensils	1:30 _____
☐ plan entertainment	☐ balloons	1:45 _____
☐ contact entertainers	☐ streamers/signs	2:00 _____
☐ buy food, décor items	☐ place cards	2:15 _____
☐ prepare house for party	☐ favors/party bags	2:30 _____
☐ decorate	☐	2:45 _____
☐	☐	3:00 _____
☐	☐	_____
☐ clean –up	☐	_____
☐ write thank you notes	☐	_____
☐ mail thank you notes	☐	_____

notes:	party info:
_____	date:_____
_____	time:_____
_____	theme:_____
_____	cake:_____
_____	favors: _____
_____	entertainment:

birthday party planner

to do:	to buy:	party schedule:
☐ select party date	☐ invitations	start _____
☐ make guest list	☐ stamps	0:15 _____
☐ address invitations	☐ paper cups	0:30 _____
☐ mail invitations	☐ paper plates	0:45 _____
☐ plan party theme	☐ napkins	1:00 _____
☐ decide on favors	☐ tablecloth	1:15 _____
☐ order birthday cake	☐ utensils	1:30 _____
☐ plan entertainment	☐ balloons	1:45 _____
☐ contact entertainers	☐ streamers/signs	2:00 _____
☐ buy food, décor items	☐ place cards	2:15 _____
☐ prepare house for party	☐ favors/party bags	2:30 _____
☐ decorate	☐	2:45 _____
☐	☐	3:00 _____
☐	☐	_____
☐ clean –up	☐	_____
☐ write thank you notes	☐	_____
☐ mail thank you notes	☐	_____

notes:	party info:
_____	date:_____
_____	time:_____
_____	theme:_____
_____	cake:_____
_____	favors: _____
_____	entertainment:

birthday party planner

to do:	to buy:	party schedule:
☐ select party date	☐ invitations	start _____
☐ make guest list	☐ stamps	0:15 _____
☐ address invitations	☐ paper cups	0:30 _____
☐ mail invitations	☐ paper plates	0:45 _____
☐ plan party theme	☐ napkins	1:00 _____
☐ decide on favors	☐ tablecloth	1:15 _____
☐ order birthday cake	☐ utensils	1:30 _____
☐ plan entertainment	☐ balloons	1:45 _____
☐ contact entertainers	☐ streamers/signs	2:00 _____
☐ buy food, décor items	☐ place cards	2:15 _____
☐ prepare house for party	☐ favors/party bags	2:30 _____
☐ decorate	☐	2:45 _____
☐	☐	3:00 _____
☐	☐	_____
☐ clean –up	☐	_____
☐ write thank you notes	☐	_____
☐ mail thank you notes	☐	_____

notes:	party info:
_____	date:_____
_____	time:_____
_____	theme:_____
_____	cake:_____
_____	favors: _____
_____	entertainment:

birthday party planner

to do:	to buy:	party schedule:
☐ select party date	☐ invitations	start _____
☐ make guest list	☐ stamps	0:15 _____
☐ address invitations	☐ paper cups	0:30 _____
☐ mail invitations	☐ paper plates	0:45 _____
☐ plan party theme	☐ napkins	1:00 _____
☐ decide on favors	☐ tablecloth	1:15 _____
☐ order birthday cake	☐ utensils	1:30 _____
☐ plan entertainment	☐ balloons	1:45 _____
☐ contact entertainers	☐ streamers/signs	2:00 _____
☐ buy food, décor items	☐ place cards	2:15 _____
☐ prepare house for party	☐ favors/party bags	2:30 _____
☐ decorate	☐	2:45 _____
☐	☐	3:00 _____
☐	☐	_____
☐ clean –up	☐	_____
☐ write thank you notes	☐	_____
☐ mail thank you notes	☐	_____

notes:	party info:
_____	date:_____
_____	time:_____
_____	theme:_____
_____	cake:_____
_____	favors: _____
_____	entertainment:

birthday party planner

to do:	to buy:	party schedule:
☐ select party date	☐ invitations	start _____
☐ make guest list	☐ stamps	0:15 _____
☐ address invitations	☐ paper cups	0:30 _____
☐ mail invitations	☐ paper plates	0:45 _____
☐ plan party theme	☐ napkins	1:00 _____
☐ decide on favors	☐ tablecloth	1:15 _____
☐ order birthday cake	☐ utensils	1:30 _____
☐ plan entertainment	☐ balloons	1:45 _____
☐ contact entertainers	☐ streamers/signs	2:00 _____
☐ buy food, décor items	☐ place cards	2:15 _____
☐ prepare house for party	☐ favors/party bags	2:30 _____
☐ decorate	☐	2:45 _____
☐	☐	3:00 _____
☐	☐	_____
☐ clean –up	☐	_____
☐ write thank you notes	☐	_____
☐ mail thank you notes	☐	_____

notes:	party info:
_____	date:_____
_____	time:_____
_____	theme:_____
_____	cake:_____
_____	favors: _____
_____	entertainment:

birthday party planner

to do:	to buy:	party schedule:
☐ select party date	☐ invitations	start _____
☐ make guest list	☐ stamps	0:15 _____
☐ address invitations	☐ paper cups	0:30 _____
☐ mail invitations	☐ paper plates	0:45 _____
☐ plan party theme	☐ napkins	1:00 _____
☐ decide on favors	☐ tablecloth	1:15 _____
☐ order birthday cake	☐ utensils	1:30 _____
☐ plan entertainment	☐ balloons	1:45 _____
☐ contact entertainers	☐ streamers/signs	2:00 _____
☐ buy food, décor items	☐ place cards	2:15 _____
☐ prepare house for party	☐ favors/party bags	2:30 _____
☐ decorate	☐	2:45 _____
☐	☐	3:00 _____
☐	☐	_____
☐ clean –up	☐	_____
☐ write thank you notes	☐	_____
☐ mail thank you notes	☐	_____

notes:	party info:
_____	date:_____
_____	time:_____
_____	theme:_____
_____	cake:_____
_____	favors: _____
_____	entertainment:

birthday party planner

to do:	to buy:	party schedule:
☐ select party date	☐ invitations	start _____
☐ make guest list	☐ stamps	0:15 _____
☐ address invitations	☐ paper cups	0:30 _____
☐ mail invitations	☐ paper plates	0:45 _____
☐ plan party theme	☐ napkins	1:00 _____
☐ decide on favors	☐ tablecloth	1:15 _____
☐ order birthday cake	☐ utensils	1:30 _____
☐ plan entertainment	☐ balloons	1:45 _____
☐ contact entertainers	☐ streamers/signs	2:00 _____
☐ buy food, décor items	☐ place cards	2:15 _____
☐ prepare house for party	☐ favors/party bags	2:30 _____
☐ decorate	☐	2:45 _____
☐	☐	3:00 _____
☐	☐	_____
☐ clean –up	☐	_____
☐ write thank you notes	☐	_____
☐ mail thank you notes	☐	_____

notes:	party info:
_____	date:_____
_____	time:_____
_____	theme:_____
_____	cake:_____
_____	favors: _____
_____	entertainment:

birthday party planner

to do:	to buy:	party schedule:
☐ select party date	☐ invitations	start _____
☐ make guest list	☐ stamps	0:15 _____
☐ address invitations	☐ paper cups	0:30 _____
☐ mail invitations	☐ paper plates	0:45 _____
☐ plan party theme	☐ napkins	1:00 _____
☐ decide on favors	☐ tablecloth	1:15 _____
☐ order birthday cake	☐ utensils	1:30 _____
☐ plan entertainment	☐ balloons	1:45 _____
☐ contact entertainers	☐ streamers/signs	2:00 _____
☐ buy food, décor items	☐ place cards	2:15 _____
☐ prepare house for party	☐ favors/party bags	2:30 _____
☐ decorate	☐	2:45 _____
☐	☐	3:00 _____
☐	☐	_____
☐ clean –up	☐	_____
☐ write thank you notes	☐	_____
☐ mail thank you notes	☐	_____

notes:	party info:
_____	date:_____
_____	time:_____
_____	theme:_____
_____	cake:_____
_____	favors: _____
_____	entertainment:

birthday party planner

to do:	to buy:	party schedule:
☐ select party date	☐ invitations	start _____
☐ make guest list	☐ stamps	0:15 _____
☐ address invitations	☐ paper cups	0:30 _____
☐ mail invitations	☐ paper plates	0:45 _____
☐ plan party theme	☐ napkins	1:00 _____
☐ decide on favors	☐ tablecloth	1:15 _____
☐ order birthday cake	☐ utensils	1:30 _____
☐ plan entertainment	☐ balloons	1:45 _____
☐ contact entertainers	☐ streamers/signs	2:00 _____
☐ buy food, décor items	☐ place cards	2:15 _____
☐ prepare house for party	☐ favors/party bags	2:30 _____
☐ decorate	☐	2:45 _____
☐	☐	3:00 _____
☐	☐	_____
☐ clean –up	☐	_____
☐ write thank you notes	☐	_____
☐ mail thank you notes	☐	_____

notes:	party info:
_____	date:_____
_____	time:_____
_____	theme:_____
_____	cake:_____
_____	favors: _____
_____	entertainment:

birthday party planner

to do:	to buy:	party schedule:
☐ select party date	☐ invitations	start _____
☐ make guest list	☐ stamps	0:15 _____
☐ address invitations	☐ paper cups	0:30 _____
☐ mail invitations	☐ paper plates	0:45 _____
☐ plan party theme	☐ napkins	1:00 _____
☐ decide on favors	☐ tablecloth	1:15 _____
☐ order birthday cake	☐ utensils	1:30 _____
☐ plan entertainment	☐ balloons	1:45 _____
☐ contact entertainers	☐ streamers/signs	2:00 _____
☐ buy food, décor items	☐ place cards	2:15 _____
☐ prepare house for party	☐ favors/party bags	2:30 _____
☐ decorate	☐	2:45 _____
☐	☐	3:00 _____
☐	☐	_____
☐ clean –up	☐	_____
☐ write thank you notes	☐	_____
☐ mail thank you notes	☐	_____

notes:	party info:
_____	date:_____
_____	time:_____
_____	theme:_____
_____	cake:_____
_____	favors: _____
_____	entertainment:

birthday party planner

to do:	to buy:	party schedule:
☐ select party date	☐ invitations	start _____
☐ make guest list	☐ stamps	0:15 _____
☐ address invitations	☐ paper cups	0:30 _____
☐ mail invitations	☐ paper plates	0:45 _____
☐ plan party theme	☐ napkins	1:00 _____
☐ decide on favors	☐ tablecloth	1:15 _____
☐ order birthday cake	☐ utensils	1:30 _____
☐ plan entertainment	☐ balloons	1:45 _____
☐ contact entertainers	☐ streamers/signs	2:00 _____
☐ buy food, décor items	☐ place cards	2:15 _____
☐ prepare house for party	☐ favors/party bags	2:30 _____
☐ decorate	☐	2:45 _____
☐	☐	3:00 _____
☐	☐	_____
☐ clean –up	☐	_____
☐ write thank you notes	☐	_____
☐ mail thank you notes	☐	_____

notes:	party info:
_____	date:_____
_____	time:_____
_____	theme:_____
_____	cake:_____
_____	favors: _____
_____	entertainment:

birthday party planner

to do:	to buy:	party schedule:
☐ select party date	☐ invitations	start _____
☐ make guest list	☐ stamps	0:15 _____
☐ address invitations	☐ paper cups	0:30 _____
☐ mail invitations	☐ paper plates	0:45 _____
☐ plan party theme	☐ napkins	1:00 _____
☐ decide on favors	☐ tablecloth	1:15 _____
☐ order birthday cake	☐ utensils	1:30 _____
☐ plan entertainment	☐ balloons	1:45 _____
☐ contact entertainers	☐ streamers/signs	2:00 _____
☐ buy food, décor items	☐ place cards	2:15 _____
☐ prepare house for party	☐ favors/party bags	2:30 _____
☐ decorate	☐	2:45 _____
☐	☐	3:00 _____
☐	☐	_____
☐ clean –up	☐	_____
☐ write thank you notes	☐	_____
☐ mail thank you notes	☐	_____

notes:	party info:
_____	date:_____
_____	time:_____
_____	theme:_____
_____	cake:_____
_____	favors: _____
_____	entertainment:

birthday party planner

to do:	to buy:	party schedule:
☐ select party date	☐ invitations	start _____
☐ make guest list	☐ stamps	0:15 _____
☐ address invitations	☐ paper cups	0:30 _____
☐ mail invitations	☐ paper plates	0:45 _____
☐ plan party theme	☐ napkins	1:00 _____
☐ decide on favors	☐ tablecloth	1:15 _____
☐ order birthday cake	☐ utensils	1:30 _____
☐ plan entertainment	☐ balloons	1:45 _____
☐ contact entertainers	☐ streamers/signs	2:00 _____
☐ buy food, décor items	☐ place cards	2:15 _____
☐ prepare house for party	☐ favors/party bags	2:30 _____
☐ decorate	☐	2:45 _____
☐	☐	3:00 _____
☐	☐	_____
☐ clean –up	☐	_____
☐ write thank you notes	☐	_____
☐ mail thank you notes	☐	_____

notes:	party info:
_____	date:_____
_____	time:_____
_____	theme:_____
_____	cake:_____
_____	favors: _____
_____	entertainment:

birthday party planner

to do:	to buy:	party schedule:
☐ select party date	☐ invitations	start _____
☐ make guest list	☐ stamps	0:15 _____
☐ address invitations	☐ paper cups	0:30 _____
☐ mail invitations	☐ paper plates	0:45 _____
☐ plan party theme	☐ napkins	1:00 _____
☐ decide on favors	☐ tablecloth	1:15 _____
☐ order birthday cake	☐ utensils	1:30 _____
☐ plan entertainment	☐ balloons	1:45 _____
☐ contact entertainers	☐ streamers/signs	2:00 _____
☐ buy food, décor items	☐ place cards	2:15 _____
☐ prepare house for party	☐ favors/party bags	2:30 _____
☐ decorate	☐	2:45 _____
☐	☐	3:00 _____
☐	☐	_____
☐ clean –up	☐	_____
☐ write thank you notes	☐	_____
☐ mail thank you notes	☐	_____

notes:	party info:
_____	date:_____
_____	time:_____
_____	theme:_____
_____	cake:_____
_____	favors: _____
_____	entertainment:

birthday party planner

to do:	to buy:	party schedule:
☐ select party date	☐ invitations	start _____
☐ make guest list	☐ stamps	0:15 _____
☐ address invitations	☐ paper cups	0:30 _____
☐ mail invitations	☐ paper plates	0:45 _____
☐ plan party theme	☐ napkins	1:00 _____
☐ decide on favors	☐ tablecloth	1:15 _____
☐ order birthday cake	☐ utensils	1:30 _____
☐ plan entertainment	☐ balloons	1:45 _____
☐ contact entertainers	☐ streamers/signs	2:00 _____
☐ buy food, décor items	☐ place cards	2:15 _____
☐ prepare house for party	☐ favors/party bags	2:30 _____
☐ decorate	☐	2:45 _____
☐	☐	3:00 _____
☐	☐	_____
☐ clean –up	☐	_____
☐ write thank you notes	☐	_____
☐ mail thank you notes	☐	_____

notes:	party info:
_____	date:_____
_____	time:_____
_____	theme:_____
_____	cake:_____
_____	favors: _____
_____	entertainment:

birthday party planner

to do:	to buy:	party schedule:
☐ select party date	☐ invitations	start _____
☐ make guest list	☐ stamps	0:15 _____
☐ address invitations	☐ paper cups	0:30 _____
☐ mail invitations	☐ paper plates	0:45 _____
☐ plan party theme	☐ napkins	1:00 _____
☐ decide on favors	☐ tablecloth	1:15 _____
☐ order birthday cake	☐ utensils	1:30 _____
☐ plan entertainment	☐ balloons	1:45 _____
☐ contact entertainers	☐ streamers/signs	2:00 _____
☐ buy food, décor items	☐ place cards	2:15 _____
☐ prepare house for party	☐ favors/party bags	2:30 _____
☐ decorate	☐	2:45 _____
☐	☐	3:00 _____
☐	☐	_____
☐ clean –up	☐	_____
☐ write thank you notes	☐	_____
☐ mail thank you notes	☐	_____

notes:	party info:
_____	date:_____
_____	time:_____
_____	theme:_____
_____	cake:_____
_____	favors: _____
_____	entertainment:

Made in United States
Orlando, FL
26 July 2023

35489525R00057